HOW
NOVELISTS
WORK

HOW NOVELISTS WORK

Edited by
Maura Dooley

Series Editor
Tony Curtis

seren

seren is the book imprint of
Poetry Wales Press Ltd
Nolton Street, Bridgend, CF31 3BN, Wales

Essays © The Authors
Editorial and Introduction © Maura Dooley, 2000

ISBN 1-85411-192-2

A CIP record for this title is available from
the British Library

*The publisher works with the financial assistance of the
Arts Council of Wales*

Printed in Plantin by CPD Wales, Ebbw Vale

Contents

Introduction: Still at the Bus Stop

People think because a novel's invented, it isn't true. Exactly the reverse is the case. Because a novel's invented, it is true.
X.Trapnel, novelist, in *Hearing Secret Harmonies* by Anthony Powell

When I first began to talk about this collection of essays, a few years ago, I was taken aback by the responses of several of the writers to whom I spoke. One novelist told me that if her agent and publisher knew the truth about the way she writes her novels (very, very quickly) they would lose all faith in her as a serious literary novelist, they would consider her a hack. Therefore, when it came to describing her working methods she would only be able to write a pack of lies, so she thought she had better not risk it.

Several others did not want to demystify the process, even to themselves, for fear that the unravelling would in some superstitious way leave them incapable of writing another novel. For those who were interested in attempting to write about it, contributing an essay seemed to present an opportunity to clarify something for themselves. Why is writing such a mysterious process and why, for some, does it seem dangerous to examine that process? Are these explorative essays inventions or are they truths? One of the contributors to the companion volume *How Poets Work* wanted to withdraw his essay, before publication, because he no longer believed what he had written six months earlier.

Writing is so personal, so subjective, so deeply and intricately threaded through, in, under, over, around a writer's life, that our ideas about where it comes from and why must change and evolve constantly. Yet here are ten essays that throw light, that engage and involve and amuse and teach us, both as readers, and perhaps if not today, then maybe tomorrow, as writers.

As the essays began to arrive I became fascinated by the web that linked them. An image would arrive fully-fledged in one contribution to flash by again in the next: for Caryl Phillips

Trying to write a novel is like waiting for a bus in the rain. A number of buses appear and pull up at the stop, but you have to know which is the one that you should climb aboard.

For Jennifer Johnston:

I am the bus into which these ideas climb and when we all reach our destination they get off and go their ways into the world. The bus is then empty and ready for its next passengers.

Something that links many of these contributions is a fascinating glimpse into where and how it all started. Adam Thorpe began his first fictions in a room at the back of the shop where his mother worked:

Now, to write a novel in the back room of an optician's, fronted by one's mother and rows of spectacles, buttressed at the back by a wild garden, strikes me as being rather memorably symbolic, but that's how it was. To write a novel is to don a different pair of spectacles, to test a different way of looking at things, and, of course, everything one writes is situated somewhere between Mum and the wild garden.

Maureen Duffy soon realised that to become a writer she must strike out on her own:

At twelve, now strongly under the influence of Keats and Milton and having passed the scholarship so that all the kingdoms of the world were in theory there before me, I decided to be a writer. Once again no one in our family had ever done such a thing and I realised I must keep it secret. Working class children, especially bastards, who were lucky enough to get to the grammar school were expected to go for security and respectability.

Maureen Duffy began with poetry and came later to drama and fiction. I too write poetry but over the years I have taken occasional experimental walks into the forest of fiction.

The first time I tried to write a novel I was seven years old and had just discovered King Arthur. My head was stuffed with visions of Guinevere, Sir Galahad, the memory of a visit to the exquisitely disappointing Cadbury Camp (no Merlin, no chocolate) and images of the Disney film *The Sword in the Stone*. I filled about twenty pages of my bright red Jumbo Winfield Jotter before losing my heart to Sindy. Three years later there followed a second novel, this time illustrated. Naturally, it involved the wardrobe interests of a group of very smart girls with big hair, outrageously high heels and improbably small waists:

> Gretchen's dress was mauve with coloured blobs on and one of those gaps in the middle. It was most peculiar. Catrina's was blue with mauve stripes. The others were nearly all plain. "As you know," said Madame, "this is a dancing competition but I have decided that you also have to make up some poetry." Everybody gasped.

As well they might. As indeed I did, when I came upon this recently and discovered I was clearly already an evangelist for poetry at the age of ten.

At fifteen, my attempted novel swiftly turned into a short story, Grand Guignol meets Dylan Thomas: a lot of crashing surf, mis-understood youth and death on the rocks. I painted a very nice frontispiece though.

In a post-university slump, far from home, I tried again. The novel was about a young woman who finds herself adrift in a strange town, in a post-university slump, and cannot see what to do with her life. I don't remember but, post-Sindy, she probably had cropped hair, flat heels and a thick waist. Hmm. Thankfully, about a third of the way through I ran out of steam and got a Proper Job. Or was it the other way around? For some years then I reverted to poetry, which has always been simply 'what I do'. For me the trouble with writing a novel is that by definition it is 'not what I do' and so even the thought of attempting such a thing becomes heroic: a mountain to be scaled.

Often the very excitement generated by discovering a favourite 'new author' cools into the kind of awe and respect that makes the idea of attempting such work oneself seem laughable; Jean Rhys, Elizabeth Bowen, James Baldwin, Anne Tyler, Gabriel Garcia Marquez, William Trevor, Alice Munro, Raymond Carver... those were some of the names that took me through my teens and into my twenties. Fiddling about with bits and pieces of prose, on the side, reading greedily, I began to try to look out for clues nevertheless. How was it done, how was an idea sustained, how did anyone have the self-belief to make such a thing possible?

At this point my world was turned upside down by the turning inside out of the very idea of what a novel might be, as Vikram Seth, Salman Rushdie, Jeanette Winterson, Toni Morrison, A.L.

Kennedy and Janice Galloway took me out of my twenties and into my thirties. In the end, I'd read with delight, shrug with bewildered admiration and write another poem.

As any would-be writer usually discovers, one of the most encouraging and illuminating courses of action to be followed is to find a published novelist, a novelist one admires, and listen to what he or she has to say.

For five years I lived at Lumb Bank, home of one of the Arvon Foundation's three centres. I worked as a Centre Director for an organisation that exists only to help the aspiring writer. Anyone reading this who is seriously interested in writing should not miss the opportunity of spending five days in glorious surroundings, with up to sixteen like-minded individuals who want to listen and absorb, write and talk.

It was at Lumb Bank that I first met the late J.L. Carr, whose name I had known for some time as a publisher of tiny, delightful chap books: snatches of A.E. Housman, selections from Wordsworth, *A Dictionary of Extraordinary English Cricketers....* The books were little compilations, illustrated often with appropriate woodcuts and engravings, sometimes overwritten and annotated in Jim Carr's own hand, printed in bright colours, stapled and sold for about twenty-five pence in a tray at the counter, like sweets. They were dips into different worlds, different lives. They were glimpses of the essence of something or someone. Each title often fabulously different from the next, lying companionably together. There were literally hundreds of them. It was an idea before its time, for, of course, Penguin did something similar, successfully, some years later, no doubt with more business acumen but with a good deal less charm.

J.L. Carr was an enthusiast. He was interested in life and in people. Somehow, in that publishing exercise lay the spirit so movingly at work in his novels. He had worked for years as a primary school headmaster and only began to publish later in life but he had never forgotten or discarded anything from his past;

> The one great thing is to assemble your resources. What have you done? Who did you meet? What do you know? Where have you been? It doesn't matter that none of it seems to fit together. You can use it all, use everything, assemble your resources.

It is what he had done himself.

The Harpole Report is about a primary school headmaster.

During the War Jim Carr was in Africa, *A Season in Sinjhi* is set in West Africa and in the front of my copy he has written: 'This was a try at writing a novel about people but using cricket as the theme (as Balzac might have used French banking!).'

That most subtle and haunting of his novels *A Month in the Country* is set just after the First World War in the Vale of Mowbray, in the North Riding of Yorkshire, remembered from his childhood.

He did not mean that we should slavishly write only of what we know but rather that our lives are rich and we should not be frightened to plunder that treasure, nor be put off by what may seem at first to be disparate, gaudily clashing elements. Listening to J.L. Carr talk, that first time, I began to see how it might be done. I began to see a path open before me. It's a different route, a different method for everyone. That is what this collection of essays shows. We can read, we can listen, we can learn and maybe one day the journey is suddenly possible, we can get on that bus, we can set off.

Adam Thorpe

Between Mum and the Wild Garden

My mother worked for many years as a receptionist/secretary in an opticians on a steep hill leading up to Chesham Station, and I would repair there often in the holidays. There was a cosy back room with an eye-test card, a peculiar little machine filled with beads which, once warmed up, made the metal of a pair of spectacles pliable, and a tiny, antediluvian kitchen filled up by its enormous sink, wooden plate-racks, the tummy-rumble boiler, and the ever-sour smell of old sponges and scrubbed board and Vim. From there you stepped out into a magic garden: until I was given a sixpence a week to clear it, it was completely throttled by old man's beard and brambles and nettles, but there were a few ancient apple trees and some sinuous brick paths I laboriously uncovered with my scythe and shears until the optician decided to save his weekly sixpence and I comprehended, very early on, the sadness of redundancy. The garden was walled and small but held the world, as gardens do.

Looking out on it, through the window of the mostly empty spectacle-repairs room, I began to write my first novel in a maroon school exercise-book. I was eleven years old. The novel was about a man who lost his hat on a rainy day, and a series of picaresque adventures were to follow as he chased it. As long as the wind kept up, I was fine: the novel proceeded. My models were the bedtime stories my older brother told me, everything I was currently reading – from the *Beezer* comic to *They Didn't Mean to Go to Sea*, and my own life – which was, I think, that of an average middle-class schoolboy of the '60s in southern England, made mildly exotic by memories of Calcutta and a brief sojourn, at around the same time, in what was then the Congo, whose troubles we eventually fled by boat.

Now, to write a novel in the back room of an optician's fronted by one's mother and rows of spectacles, buttressed at the back by a wild garden, strikes me as being rather memorably symbolic, but that's how it was. To write a novel is to don a different pair of spectacles, to test a different way of looking at things, and, of course, everything one writes is situated between Mum and the wild garden. What I found was that, after a nifty beginning on Chesham High Street, fluttering and ablaze with flags and banners for some celebration I don't recall now, and a neat introduction to Mr Potter, the owner of the errant hat, the wind refused to keep up, and I fell, by Chapter Two, into that dead zone familiar to all novelists as well as readers of *The Ancient Mariner*. The diminishing letters of the eye-test card seemed like a simulacrum of my predicament, though at eleven I didn't actually think that. I'm fabricating here. I just spent a lot of time squinting at the letters on the wall, which set off with a shout and dwindled to a whisper. My mother came through for her cup of tea and Digestive, clients seemed to laugh a lot through the closed door, and I began to feel that the card's becalmed, unyielding nature had something to do with the fact that my novel had come to an untimely stop.

Twenty-seven years later, I find myself in exactly the same situation. This summer, I have started my third novel thirty times*. After some thirty pages (the malediction of the number three) I enter the dead zone. Whatever degree of gusto I begin with, however fresh and thrilling the outset, all sails billowing and foam churning at the prow, I suddenly hit it and I know that I've had it. Some novelists would no doubt grind on, taking to the oars and moving inch by inch out of the doldrums. I give up, and start again. There are thirty ghost ships out there, all differently kitted out but with the same vague profile, to do with Africa. I've plotted it out quite carefully. I've let it all hang loose, but the African scents remain. My next novel will have something to do with Africa, I tell the eager enquirers after my creative health. And suddenly Africa looms like a vast cliff topped by impenetrable forest, and my Subject becomes anything but.

When this happens, I do as I didn't do twenty-seven years ago, in the back room of the optician's on Station Road: I give it another go, using cunning and stealth, keeping a look-out for the way that will take me in and through, as Magellan's men did at the bottom of South America. Think of it: they had spent months tacking down that vast American coast, meeting golden-eyed giants and the odd hail of arrows, seeing fires (Tierra del Fuego) and hearing strange music. But nowhere was there any break in the solid mass of land, only estuaries pouring forth fresh water. Something kept Magellan's belief going, something kept him believing that you could break through to another ocean and therefore circumnavigate the globe. I have no idea what, if anything, kept his belief intact as he approached the bottom latitudes, but when his men returned from their foray into the mass of inlets and little islands we now know as Estrecho de Magellanes, and told him how they had seen a vast expanse of water the other side, pacifically stretched to the horizon, I presume he will not have felt a sense of incredulity, but of pleasure and relief and maybe wonder. Because that's how it is when you break through to your novel and its vast, potential spaces. When you know that the trickiest bit of navigating is over, and the reason you are there at all, writing this thing, naming your space, is justified as well as clear. Now maybe if I had kept going to page thirty-five, say, the palm-fringed colossus that blocked my path might have revealed a tiny, deep inlet, and that inlet a split between two islands, and beyond that a vast, blue horizon... but I doubt it. I have not yet had, on this voyage, that Magellan faith, deep down, however much I've been assuring my wife that this was really It, this time.

And now – as the leaves are falling? I am writing poetry, and I cannot write prose fiction when I am writing poetry. The poetry Muse is a friable naiad: she flees on an impulse. She will not share the room with her sturdier counterpart, who is something of a fabulist, a *jongleur* rather than a bashful genie. But the *jongleur* has a strange habit of suddenly springing in head-over-heels from the wings, without warning. There are many imitations in my head, but they are not nearly so supple and wild.

Jongleurs and Magellans! In the writing, yes, every novel is indeed a Homeric journey, with its fresh beginnings and its adventures and its calm return to the same place but with a changed crew, maybe even only a handful of survivors, ragged and browned and waving their caps at people who hardly remember them. It must be that for the reader, too. That is the kind of novel I want to write, anyway: not the phut-phut excursion round the lake but the full-blown odyssey. This is nothing to do with length, of course. My first published work was, in fact, poetry. Poetry works vertically, and prose can too, while at the same time taking the reader *along*. The most dramatic fusion this century of the two vertical and horizontal aspects of writing, at least in English, is found in David Jones's two great works – *In Parenthesis* and *The Anathemata*. Without rhythm, verbal music, all the stuff that poets work with, prose is uninteresting. It simply passes the time. All writing concerns the ear as well as the eye. You can't have two writers more different than, say, Proust and Flaubert, yet both share an obsessive concern for what one might call 'deep style' – and Joyce learned it from them. In English, 'style' has an unfortunate connotation. So I add 'deep' to it to qualify those intimations of surface the term bears for the modern Anglo-Saxon mind. When I think of 'style', I think of illuminated manuscripts, the Lindisfarne Gospels for example, and the way in which form and content, the eye and the ear, are intimately bound one to the other. And beneath and beyond is the 'subtle body' of the work, the spirit which presses up and forms the language, and which is something to do with the author's vision. It is quite possible to have an empty work, a husk, which is nevertheless praised for its language. There are many of these around, although normally the language, the 'style', justifies our suspicion of it in these cases, because it merely decorates a void.

There are many aspects that are essential to a novel, and here's a selection as they apply to my own work.

In an ideal novel, the reader is *active*. The reader must work with the author to form the mysterious third, which is the life of the novel. Ideally, a novel should be infinitely rereadable, and each reading should bring increased enjoyment and further discoveries, like a familiar landscape one can walk day after day, and never exhaust. This is very often the case with poems, but the sheer length of the novel discourages more than a single reading. Most novels are, in fact, content with this. They are very horizontal.

The good novel must surprise, as life surprises. The temptation is for any novelist to remain one step behind life, noting things down, a Boswell to life's ebullient and slightly crazy Dr Johnson. This is the curse of *description*, encouraged in too many creative-writing classes. Of course the eye is important, and the novel in English prides itself on telling detail, the particular over the universal – but description must glance off, not pin down. It is the most difficult thing to get right. An example: in many of our most celebrated living authors, a character is introduced through head-to-toe description of his or her dress. No doubt gaining its *imprimatur* from nineteenth-century models, it sits ill with late twentieth-century ways of perceiving, and at the most basic level snares the pace of the narrative. When, say, Dickens or Flaubert do it, it is always necessary, and is part of the rich materialism of their era. These days, it is mostly the product of laziness, an inability to think through the presentation of perception. What one *leaves out* is as important as what one *includes*. For instance, Hilary Mantel's *A Place of Greater Safety* is a masterpiece of suggestion, of the barely-described, and yet leaves a vivi\d image of revolutionary France in the mind of the reader.

The two art forms peculiar to the last hundred years are film and collage. Both have changed our ways of looking at things, making us think of things cut and torn and attached. The Austrian novelist Gert Jonke has said that everything happens between the words. The meeting of any two words, phrases, paragraphs, creates a vibrancy, a surprise. A smooth narrative is made up of a million rough joins, a myriad lost words, phrases, paragraphs, in which the real life of the novel also happens. If life consists of the improbably real, then the novel – according to D.H. Lawrence, nothing less than 'the book of life' – must be equal with and to it, must keep step. An example: three days ago, in Lyon, I was saying something about all this to my French translator, who was treating me to drinks in a posh hotel. The little tray of olives and nuts he had asked for, barely touched, was suddenly whisked away and another, apparently identical, put in its place. I stopped mid-sentence, surprised even in these congenially arranged and ordered surroundings by the oddity of things. I love actions whose explanations remain barely perceptible, on the edge of the close-textured map of reasonableness we like to think surrounds us. And the waiter who had performed this beautifully mysterious action? He was a small, cadaverous young man behind his black bow tie, who explained that he had only been in England once – 'when playing rugby...'. We expressed our surprise, so he smiled and said, 'I am not all I seem'. *C'est ça.*

A novel can only surprise (as life continually does) if the author is surprised in the writing of it, which means risking surprise, taking every corner at the limits of safety, letting one's characters curl and switch and acquit themselves as they wish to.

As the novel proceeds, it stratifies, deepening its levels. Vertical, horizontal. The conjuncture of the two, the axis, is the thrilling centre of action and meaning. In the end, all that drives it is words. Such magic in words! There is an interface between the words and what they delineate; something that happens in the journey from the page into the mind's eye. My book is a cadaver of black print until a reader – bless him or her! – comes along and breathes life into it. A writer should not forget this aphasic state of the book, and the effort it takes to break that blankness. But a reader should forget what effort, what time went into the making of the sentences, because otherwise, he or she will not be enthralled. Once a reader has adjusted to my universe, I wish them to be enthralled, to be caught in the spell of the wild garden or the forest. Thinking of forests, I once knew an illiterate forester – at least, I met him in the pub a few times, a lost pub on an empty crossroads up on the Berkshire downs. He could recite a handful of complete poems, which was more than I could do after three years reading English at Oxford, but he could neither read nor write. This is how he put it to me, once: *I can read a wood*, he said, *I can open 'im up like a book*. The sadness is that most of us abuse this valuable gift of literacy; instead of reading woods, we read the conifer plantations of journalism.

Without trying to dignify my calling, I would say that it is my responsibility to offer only what is valuable, what does not waste a person's severely limited time (limited by death, I mean). It is more important to me if a hundred people feel they have spent a memorable time reading my book than ten thousand people treating it as they treat a newspaper: as something ephemeral. Of course novels change the world, as a butterfly's wing creates tornadoes, or so I understand. But that is not my primary motivation for writing them. I'm not sure what is my primary motivation. I am obsessed, driven to write. I find certain things in people's behaviour fascinating: among them, unintentional duplicity and the teetering elegance of most public behaviour. Sometimes, especially in England, on English streets even before night falls, I am confronted by the same raw mineral violence I knew at school. I think, especially then, in terms of masks and anti-masks: a skinhead recounting a happy childhood picnic, or his much-loved mother's death. There, in oscillation, is energy, is life, is whatever fires me as a novelist to set it all down.

A novel must have amplitude. There is the block-and-tackle aspect of writing and there is the real presence of the vision behind it; the two create an amplitude, like a great cathedral, which is all stresses and geometry and weight as well as the sacred space it creates and contains. A novel functions as it dumbfounds, dumbfounds as it functions. It is not inferior to life, or superior. I prefer to think of my own novels tracking life like a beast of prey, light on its paws, ready to pounce at any moment – but life is just as quick and clever, and will probably always escape. The result is not disappointment, but the exhilaration of the hunt, the intense relationship between the hunter and the hunted. When I taught mime and drama, I played a game in which two students were blindfolded and one had to catch the other within a large circle delineated by the rest of the class. All one's instincts, in the blackness, became hyper-charged. One could hear the batting of an eyelid, one's body became intelligent, one's place in space became distinct, even pithy. This is how writing a novel proceeds, for me; I am the hunter, following a scent, a sound, a presence. One's progress is so delicate. Each sentence, each paragraph, must have this discerning quality about it, that is nothing less than a creature on the track of all that is most mysterious and vital and profound.

Flabbiness is common to too much fiction. Stridency, flabbiness, small-talk. Like the Old English poet's moth, one is 'not one whit the wiser', eating those words. Even when one seeks to conjure, to imitate, the flabbiness or stridency of contemporary life, one must seek to do it *incisively*. 'The unjust walk the earth,' as Auden declared, but we do not need to be unjust ourselves. Or let me put it another way: how do we write about a woman sobbing before her shattered home? By what means do we translate the sob into more than verbal gesticulation? How do our words set themselves memorably between the quoins of the reader's imagination, so that he or she not only sees but feels the sob – sees it, as the blind Gloucester said to Lear on the blasted heath, 'feelingly'? There are two things here: there is the life to be recorded, which is nevertheless happening in my head, and the means of recording it. Each must have something totally fresh, even quirky, about it. I must not offer the soiled copy but the original, the unique. I must go beyond all received ideas and pictures of women sobbing in front of their shattered homes, and beyond the custom-built language we usually use to describe them. What is wonderful about this process is the way the thing to be set down and the means by which one sets it down are symbiotic: the word 'sob', whose origins are obscure, but which is as close to an actual sob as the language can come – this word, so close to blurring into primal sound, may well fire the image itself, make of it something completely new and strange as well as familiar. But this centripetal word converses, as it were, with all the words I choose to place around it. If I use neutral words, then it will stand out like the elaborate peak of a pommel on a well-worn saddle. If I coil and thicken the language around it, it will take its place discreetly. And above all, it will accumulate significance not only in the playing of its semantic role but in its rhythmic dynamics. Much of this conscious decision-making will go on beneath my conscious mind, of course, but all these have to be kept in play when I come to adjusting, redrafting. I have spent more than an hour on a single sentence, sometimes, tinkering. But the Zen master who waits a whole morning and then, with a sweep of his brush, paints the cherry's branch *essentially* – that is the ideal model.

Sob... words... reader. Much can go wrong on this three-stage voyage: many the vicissitudes and great the challenge. Above all, one must be careful not to dress the sob in the livery of the pretentious. The pretentious is that which muffles an inward lack, which wraps up the sobbing woman in frippery and hustles her away into the studio glare. Ideally, at the end of this metamorphic voyage, the woman remains before her ruined home, grieving. She has not gone anywhere, in the end, because you, the writer, have respected her grief. You have incarnated the pith of it.

A novel is also convivial, a great extended feast under plane trees, or around a fire. Let us not be too pious about it all. Let us be honest and sincere, but let us also laugh and tell jokes. Let us conjure the spirit of Rabelais and Sterne and the vulgar tongues of Joyce. If we are, as Guy Davenport has put it, 'gypsies camping in ruins once again', we can marvel at the comedy of our predicament. 'Art', he has also said, 'is the attention we pay to the wholeness of the world'. We do not drag out that wholeness by the scruff of the neck, and beat it about the chops, thinking it might talk that way. But neither do we keep our breath abated forever, in reverence. Fastidiousness and pedantry remain in the library, where they do very well, and where the laughter from the square bothers them, of course.

I write for a few known to me, and whom I love and respect. Beyond these I am always surprised to find others, who respond either gratefully or otherwise. The most dangerous reader is the one who reads negligently, or barely reads at all, and then writes about your book. Apart from the errors, the obvious errors, these types will compensate for their negligence with a strident critical intemperateness, a kind of bombast that tends to recoil in hatred and gives the game away. The simpleton and the smart-aleck meet happily in the mind of a reviewer. But the writer weathers it, as he or she weathers everything else – including having to review, of course.

The involuntary must be accepted, along with the inexorable. Each sentence begins with a multitude of choices, of which only one, you fear, is right. Each day you sit down with a pocketful of dragon's teeth, and you sow them, and you fight the warriors of choice. It is very fatiguing. I do this for three hours in the morning and three hours in the afternoon. I look out upon hills, where I would like to be walking. The only noises that bother me, apart from road drills and sirens (but I live in a very quiet village) are the barking of a dog and the buzzing of a fly. Both have a moronic element about them that stops me working. If a dog problem asserted itself, I would have to move. Repetition hinders the spontaneous element, the improvisatory, just as ambient recorded music – in shops, in French towns on market day, in almost any public place in the West – crushes one's own whistling or humming, one's own drum, and renders one internally mute. But the worst enemy is oneself, the part of oneself dressed in field grey, which would like everything to be predictable and perfectly behaved, and to move when shouted at. You have to pretend to be deaf, that's all.

There is the first draft, the magma, and the last draft, the little tiny flowers on the slope of the meadow. My last novel, *Still*, was written in two distinct phases, igneous and calcareous: the igneous phase took two years and was a sort of huge offshoot of the 1914 chapter in my first novel, *Ulverton*. 350 pages into this igneous phase, I realised with a dreadful clarity that I was bored stiff. My hero was about to go up to the front line of the Somme, and it was the end of June, 1916. Never work with children, horses, or people in uniform. The same day that I was bored by my own work, I read (on the same page of the *Observer*) a review of World War I novels, each of which dealt with the twin aspects of my own novel, and apparently dealt with them very well. A gunshot rang out and my novel fell, killed instantly, possibly shot for desertion. After a few days of internal crisis, during which I saw a programme on the pianist Glenn Gould, and went through the ruined house next to us for shards of former peasant lives, I sat down in my study in order to begin again. A line came into my head, so I tapped it out: *The ghosts of my grandfather, great-aunt and great-uncle rose up and they said: I don't think you have the right.* Now there were two things strange about this involuntary beginning: first, it seemed to be spookily related to my own grandfather, great-aunt and great-uncle, since the discarded 350 pages dealt loosely with their own histories; secondly, the voice that said it in my head was vaguely American, or Americanised. I decided to go with it, despite its apparent and complete unsuitability. It carried on. It mentioned a party, it began to take on a form, a character emerged, he sketched himself, he appeared to have been married twice – divorced, then a widower – and originally hailed from Enfield, though now teaching film studies in Houston. The party was very important, in some way, and was set in the near future – ah, the last evening of the millennium! He had made films in the past, with titles like *Will There's a Way* and *Honky Tonk Two*. I didn't know, as a matter of fact, that there was a *Honky Tonk* for real, but Ricky did, evidently, and had made the (dreadful) sequel. Ricky was the owner of this voice. Nearly six hundred pages later, he stopped. He had overlaid the igneous phase with his own rock. He had done incredible things with the earlier phase. He had only got to about a hundred pages in, which left the trench bits still to do, but I think that was the point: the Great War is a great void, an emptiness, a hoarse and bewildering nonsense, a dead-weight of corpse on the century's back. Gone is the time to deal with it conventionally. I think my grandfather, who apparently never talked about his time in the Somme trenches and in the slop-holes of the Ypres salient, would have agreed. My great-uncle, who was killed on the penultimate day of it, had no time to agree. Anyway, with a lot of fine-tuning, and a last, decisive cut (the first few pages *in toto*, including my cherished phantasmal beginning, following the maxim that nothing is truly valued without some loss involved), that was the novel I presented to my bemused editor.

Alas, with every blank page you are again a virgin. The only advance I have made is not wanting to sound like either Patrick White or D.H. Lawrence. My intimacy with words has of course deepened, and I can balance many more balls in the air than my single-orange days, and I have *seen* more, but I am forever haunted by the story an actor friend told me some years ago. Two celebrated elderly actors were together in the theatre on the first day of rehearsals. One approached the other and murmured in his ear, 'Glad to see they haven't rumbled you yet.'

---

* This essay was written in 1995. The novel referred to was eventually completed and published as *Pieces of Light* by Jonathan Cape in 1998.

Catherine Fisher

Belin's Hill

Quite often, it begins with a place. Years ago, I went to college in Caerleon, a sprawling Gwent village built on Arthurian legends and the fortress of the Second Augustan Legion, bits of which – the fortress, that is – poke up unexpectedly in people's gardens; substantial walls, a barracks, the surprisingly genial ring of the amphitheatre. Walking round it in all weathers, the corners of Backhall Street and Cross Street began to exhibit that oddly fictional quality that some places have; they become locations of an unknown, undiscovered narrative. Sitting on a bench in the churchyard, seeing someone come out of a house and walk down the street, you realise the story's going on here somewhere, and you are just outside it. Or this becomes the setting for books you've read, or are reading, streets and alleys resurfacing in other people's plots. Above the village is a hill-fort, crowned with trees. It's called Lodge Hill, but on old maps there's a moodier, more pagan name. Belinstock. Belin's Hill.

It was all there, all waiting. I had already decided I was going to be a novelist, and in fact had written one previous novel, sending it off and getting it back regularly from various kindly or truculent children's publishers. I'd already struggled with the difficulties of working a plot through to its end, trying to hold the various strands of it together, though each seemed to have its own vigour and want to go charging off in its own direction. I learned that the novelist is a chariot-racer, controlling his team, keeping them on track. As you write you pass by many potential stories, a constantly metamorphic plot – if A happens it will lead to B; if C happens, the story is another story.

I learned. But the book wasn't good. I had a feeling it wouldn't be, for a long time.

Then two things came along. One was a challenge, the other a nudge from the past.

Competitions are a fact of life these days for writers. Some despise them, others find them irresistible. This one was a promotion by the then Welsh Arts Council for a children's novel. It had a prize, and a closing date. Who knows which is most valuable?

About the same time I read some Arthur Machen. Machen is a difficult writer to categorize. Horror master, novelist, mystic, journalist, hack, none of these are quite right. Born in Caerleon, he spent a lonely youth in the countryside outside the village, then went to London and wrote his way through starvation and decadence to a cult respectability. His best books are *The Hill Of Dreams* and *The White People*. Both evoke the Usk valley as the haunt of numinous power, ancient, often malevolent, never safe, never really seen but vividly there, in the turning of a lane, the configuration of a skyline, or some strange psychic confrontation. Behind a stack of critical texts and an illicit KitKat in the college library it was Machen I read, and when I looked up Belin's Hill looked back at me through the window.

Machen showed me that Caerleon already had its own literary heritage; he had made another place of it, keeping some of the real village, but only the bits he wanted to keep, that served his purposes.

That's what I would do.

In *Belin's Hill* Huw and his sister Lizzie come to live in Caerleon. They explore – early drafts were burdened with loving but unnecessary description. They meet the Vicar – a nosy, rather worldly man – and Hal Vaughn, who lives in a dilapidated manorhouse on the hill. Belin's Hill begins to affect Huw strangely; he climbs up there, and later acts increasingly irrationally, until at last he goes out one night to an archeological site in the village and begins to dig in the bottom of the pit. He finds a stone head.

> Huw was suddenly still. In the mess of soil under his hands something was stirring, rising up. Lumps of soil shifted, rolled aside. In the dimness he glimpsed something pale, and stretched out his fingers reluctantly and touched it, and it was hard and cold. He heaved it up, tugged it out, feeling the soil squirm and quiver as the stone face came up, uncovered itself, earth falling from its narrow eyes, the thin gash of its lips mocking him.

The supernatural elements of the story were my main interest. Huw is haunted by the head, and by some presence on the hill; Hal by his family's curse which he feels he has to end. The climax brings the two of them together during a great fire on the hill, and Hal sacrifices himself to end the cycle.

The book was finished and I was proud of it.

It came nowhere.

Failure is never as hard to handle as success. After a few out-ings to publishers *Belin's Hill* went into a cupboard and stayed there for fifteen years. Perhaps I knew even then that its time hadn't come. In the mean time, I learned the craft. Doggedly, and for the most part, alone, because essentially that's how you do it – reading other people s work, staring ruefully at displays in book-shops, plotting, always writing. The novels – there were to be another two before any real success – firmed up, became slicker, tauter. Lessons learned from poetry went into them, the importance of cutting, of the sharp phrase, of not wasting time. In children's books, I discovered, story is everything and as I went on I could feel the strength of the narratives pulling me harder.

The Conjuror's Game was published in 1990, mainly as a result of acquiring an enthusiastic agent who knew exactly where the markets were. By this time, anyone's enthusiasm was disconcerting, almost unnerving – to see the book in print and short-listed for a major prize was scary. Suddenly it mattered what you wrote. People noticed. Reviews were written. It was all much more serious.

Publication sobers you up. It also gives a dangerous confidence. The novels began to come more readily – *Fintan's Tower*, the *Snow-Walker Trilogy*, *The Candleman*. By now the writing process was routine, fitted around a full-time, and later part-time, job. The idea – sparked by a place, picture, character – is jotted down and mulled over, often while the previous book is being finished. Other things accrue – symbols, folklore motifs, snatches of dialogue on backs of envelopes, situations, motives, names. Sometimes the title comes early, sometimes not till half-way through. The first draft is hand-written, heavily scored, with minimal forward plan-ning, just an idea to work with and see what becomes of it, but in every book there comes a time, about two-thirds of the way through, when it all threatens to stagnate, and then I have to take a clean sheet of paper and map out the end, coldly, trying to ignore intriguing diverse possibilities. Typed, edited, typed again. And not until then does anyone else see it.

All the books have a strong fantasy or supernatural element. This and an obsession with action are two of the excuses to write children's books, though the main interest for me comes in follow-ing out the story, not in guessing which age-group will read it. It was sometime near the end of the *Snow-Walker* trilogy that I took out the old *Belin's Hill* manuscript and read it again. The style was overwritten, the description laid on with a trowel, but it was then I began to see how the book should be. It would be a strange restoration, like working on a palimpsest where the earlier text still showed through. I would have to completely re-write, keeping the best parts, losing a lot, altering most. Above all, now I could see where the gaps were.

It's a commonplace of this sort of fantasy that something in the character's lives interlocks with the supernatural; this was what had been missing, the psychology of Huw's actions. Once I had found the tragedy in his recent past, the death of his parents in a train crash, all his actions – sleepwalking, flashbacks, the bizarre digging in the pit – became plausible. Suddenly I knew what the book was about. And it provided me with a new and potent symbol – the tunnel.

> The wall of the tunnel was right up against his face, so close in the darkness that he could put out his tongue and lick the damp bricks, the salts among the ferns. Water trickled against his cheek, soaking his torn shirt. For hours he stared at the ferns; they were tiny, and pale, growing in the dark, on nothing, and behind them there was a numb, distant pain somewhere deep in his skull, and a silence full of echoes, crashing echoes that reverberated for miles down the crumpled wreckage of the train.

The imagery of the book strengthened – earth and fire, the pit, the tunnel, the inferno. Entrances to the Underworld. And of course the stone head, that most enigmatic of Celtic images. Another added section to strengthen the psychology was Hal Vaughn's encounter with the ghost whose curse has destroyed his family. The aim here was to create a different tension in the reader; is she real, or is Hal's hereditary mental fragility affecting him?

> A bird fluttered in the window, catching his eyes, and he saw deep among the leaves a face looking back at him, reflected in a broken pane, a narrow face, dark and lost. For a moment he saw himself, mirrored between the ivy leaves; then the window banged with a slam that made him jump; glass slid and tinkled on the floor, a shiver of disintegrating light.

What is reality anyway? Is what we imagine as true really true for us? An intriguing aspect of the developing plot was how far this

could be taken; could every supernatural event be seen as a pro-
jection of the characters' fears and griefs – the terrible stone face
that Huw hides and buries and cannot get rid of, or Hal's ghost
who is only a breeze rocking a chair or his own reflected face?

Children's books need tension. One of the strengths of the original book was its undeniable suspense at the end. This had to be
kept, and not diluted. Short sentences became shorter, almost
breathless, as if the reader too is climbing Belin's Hill, struggling
to the book's deliberately abrupt end.

When it was finished, it had become something new. It was
finally published. And, success or failure, I knew its time had
come.

Mark Illis

Obsessive Behaviour

How Did I Start?

In my second novel, *The Alchemist*, my winning and hopeful but partly doomed young hero, Billy, writes a story in school at the age of about 11. He doesn't finish it, and has to continue it at home. That's what happened to me. I began something in class and took it home and carried on, and it finished up, I think, thirteen pages long, which as far as I was concerned was like *War and Peace*. I drew a cover for it too, which was probably no worse than some of the covers my published work has had. In the book Billy goes on to eat a torn-off piece of newspaper, in the hope that this will somehow imbue him with a writer's qualities. This whole area is difficult and subjective, but one thing I feel I can safely say is that I did not become a writer by eating newsprint.

Having parents who read, and encourage reading, and make books look like fun, is all any writer needs to start them off. It seems quite wrong that there is such a thing as a bookworm, but not a TV-worm. Books do not necessarily go hand in hand with social inadequacy. Trips to the library with my father were a pleasure, and getting P.G. Wodehouse books as a present might initially have been disappointing, but turned out to be great. I can't imagine what my life would be like without reading. The only drawback I can think of is that this early and enthusiastic introduction might be why I never read in a systematic way, why there are so many large gaps in my reading: I still expect it to be fun. I am lazy.

Other writers worry me. Apart from the fact that they seem to manage their careers better, get better paid jobs, bigger advances and more publicity, what is most annoying is that they often seem to be unreasonably clever. I know writers who are not only fantastically well-read, but also have superb memories. I'm hugely impressed by this, and jealous of it. Ian Duhig, Geoff Dyer, Will

Self, are all examples. (Possibly it's more of a male thing, related
to that mildly autistic male habit of spotting things and collecting
things, in this case books and their contents. None of these writers
actually wear anoraks, although one of them does claim to know
all the lyrics of all Bob Dylan songs.) I'm not very well-read, and
I have a bad memory. I've read too many thrillers and too much
science fiction to be really well-read, I don't have a great love like
Raymond Williams or James Joyce, or a love-hate relationship
with Freud, just a lot of shallow, average-sized enthusiasms. If
really pressed to name a favourite writer I'd probably say Dickens,
and I haven't even read all of his work.

The first reading I can remember is Enid Blyton, the *Famous
Five*, with the girl called George and the dog. I read *The Hobbit*
and loved it, was scared stiff by the giant spiders in Mirkwood,
and then, at nine or ten, read *The Lord of the Rings*. I very nearly
gave up after the first couple of chapters, but I struggled on with
it, and got into it, and before long I was loving that too. This was
my first experience of reading as sometimes requiring effort, of
that effort being well repaid, of the great pleasure of being in the
midst of a long book that draws you into its world, of reading
slowly as the end approaches, not wanting the experience to finish.

Then the Americans got me. First *The Great Gatsby*, then the
rest of Fitzgerald, then Salinger, then Faulkner, the difficult entry
into his world, the sense of ownership that developed as I got to
know his characters in different books, began to cope with his
style, recommended him to friends who said they didn't like him.
Updike, Bellow, Malamud. Hardy, Dostoevsky and Balzac, through
school and my father, and Wodehouse making his appearance
that Christmas. And always thrillers and science fiction too, trips
to the Oxfam shop, coming back with piles of Alistair Maclean,
Desmond Bagley, Asimov, but also more interesting stuff, like Le
Carré, Arthur C. Clarke, Philip K. Dick.

All of it is influence. Alistair Maclean as well as Saul Bellow,
Dickens as well as one of my current favourite writers, Don
DeLillo. Holden Caulfield's tired old adolescence still moves me,
and the overblown romanticism of Fitzgerald still has some sort
of effect. Influence begins as imitation, and it was the short stories
of Salinger and Hemingway I had in mind when I started writing.
But as my reading widened so my sense of what was possible
widened. *Money*, *A Child in Time*, *The Passion* and *The
Handmaid's Tale* were some of the outstanding novels of the 80s

for me, the time when I started getting published. They helped to show me what might be done with language and character and genre, and how one might engage with the world.

My reading has continued always to be wide but unsystematic, its influence in any case limited by my bad memory. Unlike other writers I've met, I know very little literature by heart. Scraps of Walt Whitman for instance ('Do I contradict myself? Very well then, I contradict myself'), and John Donne ('At the round earth's imagined corners, blow Your trumpets angels and arise, arise From death, you numberless infinities of souls'). Stirring stuff, but of limited relevance.

I don't know how memory works. At school we were given large chunks of Shakespeare, and the whole of the Donne sonnet beginning *Death be not proud...* to learn, but I don't remember those at all. They are presumably floating around my brain some-where, in some dusty back room, perhaps along with everything else I've ever read which has just fizzled away like steam. I have a good short-term memory when I need it, useful for exams, but my long-term memory seems almost non-existent. Not having a mental filing cabinet of useful lines to rifle through, and needing an epigraph for *The Alchemist*, I had a look in a dictionary of quotations, and came up with something that seemed appropriate:

A cheat, a thief, a swearer and
blasphemer, who smelt of the rope from
a hundred yards away, but for the rest
the best lad in the world.

It's from Clément Marot's *Epitres*, as you probably know, and it is apt, since duality is at the heart of the novel, and my young hero does some very unheroic things, but it felt like cheating to have to look it up.

After writing that story when I was eleven, I just kept going. I mostly got good marks for stories I did at school, mostly enjoyed writing the ones I did at home. In the two years after school and before university, I wrote some bits and pieces of diary-style fiction, and some pretty awful attempts at poetry, but it was when I got to UCL that I really got going.

Something good happened there. I had excellent tutors, two of whom were Karl Miller (then editor of the *London Review of Books*), and the novelist Dan Jacobson. Both were willing to read and criticise my stories, possibly more interested in them than in my essays. While I was there I entered the Whitbread Young Writers competition, and was one of the runners-up, which meant I was published by Hamish Hamilton. Twelve of us, in a book which probably sold about twelve copies. Still, a real book which had reviews, and entailed meeting editors. The story was called 'Loomis', and was a melodramatic, over-written piece about betrayal and the unreliability of heroes. But the story rattled along, and in amongst the over-writing there were probably some quite nice images. Two more stories were published while I was at UCL, and then I got a place on the Creative Writing MA at the University of East Anglia.

Good things continued to happen. I wrote my first novel at UEA, and again received excellent criticism – this time from my fellow students, and from Malcolm Bradbury and the late Angela Carter, who were running the course at the time.

When I first went to Angela's house for a tutorial, I turned into her road, a long one in Clapham with tall terraced houses on either side, and knew immediately where she lived. Hers was the only purple house on the street. There was a storm rattling as I entered, and when I went into the sitting room where she was perched on the edge of the sofa, all in black, with her pale face and cloud of white hair, there was a crash of thunder and a slash of lightning. 'Sorry,' she said, and then laughed. The room was exactly as it should have been, cluttered, with a gaudy but shabby merry-go-round horse catching my eye. She appeared distracted, and made me talk about the story I had sent her as if reminding herself, but then asked acute questions which removed any complacency I might have been developing.

Plenty of reading, some good luck at university, the famous East Anglian MA in creative writing. It would be nice to have had a more eventful background, and there are a couple of fairly devastating personal milestones along the way, but there is nothing a publicist would find sexy. A lot of writers seem to take pleasure in filling the little biographies in their books with unusual or unglamorous jobs. Something involving funerals and embalming is always popular (you're wacky, unconventional), macho pursuits like deep-sea fishing sometimes appear (you're rugged and, probably, gruff), and horny-handed, man-of-the-people jobs like road sweeping are good for credibility, (you wish you were James Kelman but, unfortunately, you aren't).

Paul Watkins, who I think wrote four books by the time he was

thirty, (to my three), and won some prizes, and went to Eton and
somewhere called the Dragon school, and travelled a lot, and got
compared to Hemingway so much it must have become irritating
for him, wrote an autobiography called *Stand Up Before Your God.*
I suppose it seemed to have a ring to it. I haven't read the book,
so I don't know exactly what the title means, but it certainly
suggests an attitude. Leaving aside all question of the quality of
our respective works, this may be why for a while he attracted
publicity like a Prime Ministerial sex scandal: the phrase 'Stand
Up Before Your God' speaks to Paul Watkins in some way. 'Sit
Down Before Your TV' has more resonance for me. 'There's A
Good Film On Later'. My feeling is, you don't have to have a
thrill-filled life to write interesting fiction. I'm not working class
and didn't go to Eton. I haven't travelled an unusual amount, or
tried any exotic jobs. I'm not an ex- or current drug addict or a
recovering alcoholic, I don't fly into rages, I'm not promiscuous
with men or women or animals, I'm possibly the straightest person
I know.

So there's not much that any publicist can say about me. Why
did I start writing? Because I wanted to. Needed to, really,
because interspersed with over-written, awkwardly-phrased stories
and clichéd, portentous poems were urgent, adolescent rushes of
unfiltered angst flowing messily out on to the paper. And the
more I poured emotion on to the page, the more I thought about
the way I was doing it, and how I might make it sound better, and
communicate more effectively. And as I became more aware of
the subtleties and choices of technique and craft, so my subject
matter began to develop.

What do I write about?

I think my subject-matter started with the typical young man's
sort of area: sex, loneliness, obsessive behaviour, but it has grown
from there. I'm interested in the meaning of masculine, in thugs,
train-spotters and new men. And in the meaning of feminine, and
how the two things relate to men and to women, because we are
living in the midst of change. I'm interested in communication,
how difficult it is to talk meaningfully and truthfully to people,
and whether it is very often desirable to do so. I'm interested in
knowing other people, how difficult it is to do that. In change,

how a child changes into a different person, an adult, and in whether an adult can choose to change again, how choice interacts with circumstance and genes. In finding a way of living in this world, accommodating its horribleness, compromising over many different areas in order not to be depressed all the time. In reflecting that world in my work, creating what Paul Auster calls 'fiction as strange as the world we live in'. In what you have to do to live a life you will think is worthwhile, if you die tomorrow, or in fifty years time. I'm also interested in character. Also in telling a story, one that will make the reader want to turn the page. (Because I don't think he or she will do so in order to discover my thoughts on gender.) Also in place and dialogue, and simply in language. We live in language, like fish in water, and I like to splash around in it a little. Fiction is about all of the above, and other preoccupations which are less important to me, or which I haven't developed yet. And it's about entertainment, and joy.

Write about what you know is a lazy cliché, but for me it makes sense, and it means most of the above. Not just my experience, but what I care about, what is central to me. That's why writing for a market tends to produce formulaic stuff without soul, because it involves writing in a cold, calculated way, looking outside instead of inside. The writer should always be looking outside and inside simultaneously, to more or less quote Scott Fitzgerald. The best genre writers are writing about what they care about, and challenging themselves and stimulating themselves. So are the best writers of literary fiction.

It doesn't mean that most novels are autobiographical, although most readers probably won't believe this. But a writer's experience will inevitably inform the writing.

My first novel, *A Chinese Summer*, was about the aftermath of a relationship, about someone who gets cancer, and about a movement from depression and isolation towards a sense of community and belonging in the personal and in the wider world. Like many first novels it was a short, first-person piece in which the narrator was the same sex and the same sort of age as the writer. And lived in the same place as the writer, and travelled on the same trains, and shared some of the same experiences. But he wasn't the writer. No, honestly. He was like the writer, but reacted to things differently, saw a skewed kind of poetry in the everyday, and suspected a conspiracy in the shape of the world around him. And his experiences were different too.

I could trace creatively-processed aspects of my own life in much of my work, but I don't really want to try. There seems nothing to be gained, and possibly something to be lost, in too thorough an examination. I don't start from my own life. I don't start from an idea. I start from character.

Structure and Method

Recently I had a full-time job, and I squeezed writing around its edges, mostly in the early mornings. The job was good but the writing suffered, so I've now given up the job. For me, full-time writing means sitting at my desk around 9 am and staying there till lunch. I don't aim to produce a certain number of words, just to work for a certain number of hours. Although I'll sometimes feel I've achieved nothing, I believe that no writing time is wasted time. Thinking about and around a problem usually brings me closer to its solution. I work best in the mornings, when I have more energy and there's nothing much else on my mind, and afternoons tend to be scrappier. Still, I'll try to return to my work for another three or so hours, perhaps spending more time on revision. Or I may be writing something like this, or preparing some teaching, or watching a repeat of *Coronation Street*.

When I am beginning a novel my first thoughts are about its main character. I start to write notes about him (so far it always is a man), and after a while the notes start to include his family, and people who know him. This begins to link in with an idea of theme and plot, and it all grows together and begins to develop some detail, some individual scenes, many of which may later be discarded, and finally some shape. Pages of notes have accrued by this time, some of them illegible, none of them in any kind of order. It's an exciting stage, because I'm full of ideas, most of which seem brilliant. It's a time when conception hasn't yet been sullied by execution, when I can almost believe that this is going to be the highly-praised, mega-selling, breakthrough, prize-winning, film-adapted, sequel-spawning, enduring classic that I know I have in me. It's a brief period, soon interrupted by steep down-ward mood-swings as I start to try to shape the growing, still largely formless, Quatermass-like heap of material.

Shaping is an almost literal term. The pages of notes are put into some kind of order. Sometimes things are stuck on the walls,

key scenes or developments. A piece of paper might be divided
into three or more parts, and different things put into different
columns. Then arrows criss-cross it, different colours are used,
and then the whole thing is screwed up and replaced.

And by now I am getting ideas for a first chapter, and beginning to want to write it. I resist this. Keep trying to get my notes
in order and get a good sense of what should go where, but the
pressure by now is building, and finally I'll just start, and write a
chapter which I hope is informed with a sense of the novel's
theme and future shape, and introduces the main character and
gets the reader's attention, and displays my distinctive voice at its
finest. And then later on I'll bin it and start at Chapter Two.

Once the writing starts, the rewriting starts. It's a question of
finding a balance between obsessively returning to what I've just
done and changing it, so that I never progress, and leaving everything to come back to, so that when I start a second draft I find
everything incredibly sloppy.

These are three versions of a passage in a novel I started a
while ago. It describes Ash and his friends discovering and claim-
ing the building they are going to make their own. (The page
numbers refer to my typescript.)

FIRST DRAFT

The beginning of the second chapter, page four of the novel.

> They had only moved in to the decrepit building, they always
> reminded Leisure Services, after it had been empty for more than
> six months. And it wasn't as if tenants were eager to look at the
> place. It was that time, that long time, when no one was buying
> and those who were renting were picking and choosing and
> stalling and haggling. No one was moving. Our properties aren't
> moving, the estate agents said. The buildings stood heavy and
> still, placid, like great, sleepy animals. And in the stillness Ash and
> Max and the rest just slipped in one morning. One day the build-
> ing was empty, and the next day it wasn't.

SECOND DRAFT

*Halfway through the second chapter, related as a flashback. Page 11
of the novel.*

> It was a damp, silent place. It was decrepit, and had been empty

for about a year. No one went there. When does moving house become breaking and entering? It was that time, that long time, when no one was buying and people who were renting were picking and choosing and stalling and haggling. No one was moving, *Our properties aren't moving,* the estate agents said. So the buildings were sitting there, not moving, like big, sleepy mammoths. And in the stillness Ash and Max and Jim just slipped in on January the first. One day the building was empty, and the next day it wasn't.

THIRD DRAFT

Page one of the novel. The Prologue.

The sky one bulging grey cloud, the temperature somewhere around zero. Max jemmied the door, and stale air greeted them. It was that time, that long time, when no one was buying. *Our properties aren't moving,* estate agents said. Sure enough, the building was still sitting there, not moving, like a big, sleepy mammoth. And in the stillness Ash and Max and Jim just slipped in with their hangovers on January the first. One day the building was empty, the next day it wasn't.

The first draft involves exposition. I'm not yet familiar with the story, and seem to be explaining it to myself. Much of the prose is clogged and slow, although the last sentence seems direct and effective. The second draft cleans up the style a little, but it has no energy. This is an important scene, and it's being thrown away in a flashback. There's too much about renting. The third draft, The Prologue, works better. A punchy opening paragraph, now opening the door on the whole novel, a mention of hangovers to reinforce the January firstness of the scene, and to provide the first dab of character for Ash, Max and Jim.

There is something very attractive about the apparatus of the novel. Title, dedication, acknowledgments, epigraph, contents page, prologue, part one, part two, part three. Not particularly because these things draw attention to the fictionality of the novel, in a postmodern, Tristram Shandy-ish way, but because there is a real pleasure in using this apparatus, as well as a practical purpose. Structure is always a challenge, but especially so in first novels, and dividing the book into chapters and/or parts helps to make sense of the material, helps to impose some sort of workable time-scale, helps to make it readable. The narrator may well be unreliable, but the writer cannot afford to be, the writer has to gain the reader's confidence early on, and keep it. The apparatus helps the writer to stay in control, and can be like a series of clues, leading the reader in the direction you want him or her to go.

Titles should work in the same way. I like titles. *A Chinese Summer*, *The Alchemist*, *The Feather Report*. I usually get them early on, and then they help me to write the book, reminding me of the controlling theme, the controlling image, the thing that everything else refers back to. Other ideas will appear, but will be rejected. They're important, but they're not at the centre. When you know you've got the right title, you know you've got into the intimate relationship with your novel that you need.

Why Write?

It's frustrating, pays terribly, encourages professional jealousy, depression, despair, insecurity, self-doubt and self-loathing. So why do it? It's true that when it's going well, writing is better than most things. It's not really better, in the moment of doing it, than having a good meal, reading a good book, seeing a good film. It's as good as those things, but not better. So why do it? There is a large cliché hurtling towards me now and there is no way of avoiding it: I have to do it. I'm unhappy if I don't do it. It's not just what I do, it's what I am.

If you feel that way, then read books like this, and go on courses if you feel the need for the time and space and advice they can provide, but mostly just read a lot, and keep writing, shaping it, working at it, making it better.

Penelope Fitzgerald

Daisy's Interview

If the subject is how, rather than why, then I think you have to distinguish between male and female novelists. I believe that most women will always be kitchen table writers and worse still that they become irreversibly conditioned to it. Just as Napoleon, if he had ten minutes to spare, allowed himself to go to sleep for ten minutes exactly, so a woman, in my experience, can pick up her draft novel and go on with it, precisely until the telephone, the door-bell, the egg-timer or the alarm clock rings. Women adapt in a peculiar way to the battle against Time and Nature. I started writing during my free periods as a teacher in a small, noisy staff-room, full of undercurrents of exhaustion, worry and reproach, and for a long time after I gave up my day-job I missed the staff-room, and, sitting in peace and quiet, could scarcely get anything written. I had thought of both of them – peace and quiet – as the absence of certain things. That's not so, they are positive, but to my dismay I found they worked against each other. In the tranquillity of my own room, overlooking a garden with a large pear-tree, I found I was waiting obsessively for an interruption and even ready to welcome it.

The patron saint of all kitchen-table novelists must be Margaret Oliphant (1828-1897) – Mrs Oliphant, as she always called herself. I once wrote the introductions for five of her novels for Virago, and in that way got to know her. She married an invalid artist cousin, for whom, if we read about him, we feel distinctly sorry – but, however that may be, he died of TB, leaving Margaret Oliphant pregnant, with nothing much beyond his debts. She paid these off, raised her children, saw every one of them die, and made herself responsible for her alcoholic brother and numerous other relations. In consequence she had to write at night ('I, too, work hard, Mrs Oliphant,' Queen Victoria told her), usually to pay off money which had already been spent. She wrote 98 novels, 25 biographies, about 50 short stories, some of them strikingly good. (I've taken these figures from Elisabeth Jay's

Mrs Oliphant: A Fiction to Herself (Oxford, 1995).) When her friend James Barrie said that 'she was of an intellect so alert that one wondered she ever fell asleep', he was poeticising an almost frightening way of life.

Mrs Oliphant, of course, had no mechanical help of any kind, only keeping a small container of prepared ink into which she put a few drops of water, enough for each night's work. On the other hand, she took for granted one great advantage of the nineteenth century writer – that is, a constant supply of listeners. These were nieces, second cousins, friends' daughters, some of them apparently living in the house and all of them ready to give their opinion when she wanted to read what she had just written aloud. That, I've always felt, would be of considerable help. But I can't tell, it's an experience I've never had.

Before I start on a novel I don't need a synopsis of what is going to happen, but I do need the title, the opening paragraph, and the last one. Once I've got these, I can start.

In 1990 a book of mine came out called *The Gate of Angels*. It was one of those novels which starts from a persistent, even obsessive, idea or image (the famous example would be George Eliot's *Silas Marner* – she called it 'a story which came across my other plans by a sudden inspiration, a sort of legendary tale, suggested to me by having once, in early childhood, seen a linen weaver with a bag on his back'). The image that stayed with me wasn't – though they so often are – from childhood. It was something I saw on a visit to Cambridge, through the window of a bus, somewhere near Newnham. It was a tremendously windy day, and on one of Cambridge's unexpected patches of green land there were cows moving about under the willow trees – the wind had torn great wreaths and branches off the willows and thrown them down to the ground. The cows were ecstatic – they were prancing, almost dancing – they'd hoped all their lives to get at the trees and now at last they could – and it struck me that in this orderly University city, the headquarters of rational and scientific thinking, things had suddenly turned upside down, reason had given way to imagination.

It happened that I had been wondering what exactly was meant by the term 'Mach 2'. I knew that it was a measure of supersonic speed and I thought it was named after a distinguished scientist, but I didn't know who Mach was, and certainly didn't realise that he was an opponent of Rutherford and the early atomic physicists because he considered that atoms were only a provisional idea; they were unobservables, and science shouldn't be based on the unobservable, otherwise it was no better off than metaphysics, which asks us to speculate about the unseeable. While I was trying to think about this, with the image of the cows and the willow-trees intervening, a novel suggested itself, turning on the problem of body and soul. The title would be *The Unobservables*. But the publishers, or rather their sales department, rejected this immediately as lacking not only in sex but in human appeal of any kind. I changed it to *Mistakes Made by Scientists*, which I liked almost as much, but I was told, quite correctly, that it wouldn't fit on the jacket and didn't sound like a novel anyway.

On this one occasion, then, I had to work without a title. Still, my attempts to find out more about Ernst Mach (1838-1916) had put me into the right period, that is the time just before the First World War when (in Cambridge in particular) there was a fierce debate between scientists and metaphysicians. I imagined Fred – representing the mind and reason, though only partly – as a young physicist during the glorious early experimental years at the Cavendish, and Daisy as a strong young woman training to be a hospital nurse. Of course, they wouldn't be anything like precise opposites. To start with, both of them would be young and poor, though Fred's would be the poverty of a shabby country vicarage and Daisy would come from teeming South London.

Daisy is a fearless survivor, a favourite type with the late Victorian and Edwardian light novelists – W.W. Jacobs, for instance, or Barry Pain in *Eliza*. Men don't disconcert these girls, nor do the regulations and prohibitions men make. In the following bit of dialogue Daisy is waiting her turn for an interview with the matron of a great London hospital, the Blackfriars. A notice on the inner door reads: 'This hospital turns away more than a thousand applications a year from persons desiring to train as nurses. Every year perhaps 4 or 5 are accepted.'

A Few Remarks on the First Draft

This is the 'catechism type' of dialogue, on which Joyce declared he based his *Portrait of the Artist as a Young Man*, where one side has the right answers and the other sometimes knows them and sometimes has to guess them. It's also a confrontation where the reader is asked to have some sympathy at least with both sides.

At the beginning I see that I hadn't really settled Daisy's age (or even her height). The qualifying age for probationers at that time was over 20, but that was too old for Daisy, who is going to act with the rashness and curiosity of a very young girl, so in the text I've made the hospital (not very probably) alter its admission policy. I've done this as unobtrusively as possible, as readers are very quick to notice this kind of mistake.

1.20 The distinction between 'lady nurses' and ordinary probationers is characteristic of the early 1900s and I wanted to get it in somewhere, but this wasn't the place to do it. The matron would have seen immediately that Daisy was 'of the domestic servant class.'

1.28 'This was not quite true.' The concept of absolute scientific truth – Fred, the physicist, holds it, and so does the matron – is totally different from Daisy's. Her idea of truth is relative, and largely depends on her own convenience and the wish not to hurt other people's feelings. This is important to the story, but it's not the moment to hold up the dialogue.

1.41 'You should call me Matron'. The matron ought to have said this much earlier. She detects the independent streak in Daisy and must make it as clear as possible from the beginning that there is no place for it in the running of a great hospital.

1.63 '(TEST here)'. A mistake. Quite out of place for Matron to make a random test at an interview, or indeed at any time.

1.65 'I need them now'. I left this in because it's not meant as a sentimental reflection, only as a warning to an ignorant girl.

At the end, however, as I saw as soon as I read it over, the dialogue goes completely to pieces. I got the question 'Have you ever been present at a death or a birth?' out of one of the numerous handbooks published around 1912-14 on the nursing profession. It has a certain force, but it's wrong here, and so is Matron's 'my dear' at 1.86. The two women must end, as they began, as adversaries who feel respect for each other, but nothing more (or less) than that. Daisy finishes 'down', but not down and out. No-one ever gets the better of Daisy except herself, or rather her own weaknesses.

All this seems like paying far too much attention to an unimportant passage. But as I'm a hopelessly addicted writer of short books I have to try to see to it that every confrontation and every dialogue has some reference to what I hope will be understood as the heart of the novel. As I've tried to explain, it's about body, mind and spirit.

Daisy was the last to be called. She looked with respect at the woman sitting on the other side of the desk. You had to struggle, perhaps fight and bleed, to get to a position like that. Matron was short, pale and pale-haired, as straight as though suspended from a hook.

'You may sit down.'

She repeated from the application paper in front of her Daisy's name and address.

'You are nearly eighteen. Are you a single woman or a widow? If you are a widow, have you children? If children, how are they provided for?'

'I'm single.'

'And have you anyone dependent on you for support?'

'Not now.'

'You may call me Matron.'

'Not now, Matron.'

'But recently?'

'There was my mother. She died in March.'

'And that left you free to apply to enter the nursing profession, which of course would entail your living away from home.'

'I suppose it did.'

'So that her death has been release for you.'

'No, I won't say that, and I don't say that. It wasn't a release for her either.'

The matron appeared not to listen to this, but fixed her attention on the papers on her desk. 'Your birth certificate. You're too young, but the Governors have changed their policy about that to some extent. Vaccination certificate.

71

The Gate of Angels

Height?' Daisy said she thought five foot six, without heels. 'It's not a matter of thinking,' the matron said. 'Educated at the Victuallers' School, certificate of good conduct and application. Did you study Latin? Do you understand what I mean by enemata?'

Daisy did not, but said she was prepared to learn.

'I don't expect the girls who come to us to know anything. Now, are you strong and healthy, and have you always been so? Let me explain, in order to save time, that several of the applications today mentioned, apparently only as an after-thought, that they had rheumatic fever as children, which meant that if they were accepted here they might collapse and become a nuisance and an expense at any given moment.'

'I've always been strong and healthy,' said Daisy and beneath her put-on clothes she felt her physical self-respect extend and stretch itself, like a cat in the sun.

'And your sight and hearing are perfect?'

'Yes, I think so. I've never thought about them.'

'You notice that I wear reading-glasses myself. I need them now, but as a probationer I did not need them. Have you any physical defects?'

'What kind of defects?' Daisy asked, a little troubled.

'Any that I can't see at a cursory glance. You may be subject to very heavy periods. You may be marked and scarred. Your spine may be crooked. . . . Have you any tendency to pulmonary complaints?' She looked up sharply. 'Do you understand what I mean by "pulmonary"?'

'Yes, it means to do with the lungs.'

'Pertaining to the lungs. A sickly nurse is of no use to the profession. One might call her an enemy of the profession. Above all, though, we don't want a weakly habit of constant complaint. As a rough guide, remember that while the average man is ill for four days a year, a grown woman must expect to spend one fourth of her life in actual pain.'

Daisy felt a rush of admiration. So far she herself had done nothing like her fair share.

FIRST DRAFT

1 Daisy's turn came; she was the last to be
2 called; the last of the 1000, perhaps. She
3 looked with respect at the woman, ~~neither~~
4 ~~young nor old,~~ sitting at the other side of
5 the desk who could scarcely have got there
6 without a ~~tough~~ prolonged struggle. [The]
7 Matron was small and sandy-haired and sat
8 up as straight as though suspended from a hook.
9 [You may sit down] she repeated from the piece
10 of paper in front of her Daisy's name and address
11   Are you a single woman or a widow? If
12 you are a widow, have you children? If children
13 how are they provided for?
14   I'm single, Daisy said.
15   ~~You are twenty-two.~~
16   And have you anyone dependent on you for
17 support?
18   Not now—
19   What was your last occupation? You under-
20 stand that we ~~have a number of gentlewomen~~
21 ~~applying here for training. There seems to~~
22 ~~be a certain fashionable craze in that respect.~~
23 ~~Of course they would not be asked to undertake~~
24 ~~any disagreeable tasks. Our staff nurse are~~
25 ~~drawn mainly from the domestic service class~~
26   I'm ~~not a gentlewoman~~ Daisy said but I've
27 ~~never been in service either~~
28   ~~That was not quite true There had been the~~
29 ~~washing-up job at seven shillings a week, with~~
30 ~~threepence held back for breakages~~
31   Your age last birthday? You are still only
32 ~~18~~ ~~22~~ 17? Your vaccination certificate? Your
33 height? Daisy said she thought five foot four,
34 without heels. It's not a matter of thinking the
35 Matron said. Where were you educated? —
36 I went to the elementary, ~~then I had the~~
37 ~~council scholarship~~ then I went to the Victuallers
38 school. — And you have a certificate of good
39 conduct and application?
40 Yes ma'am
41 You should call me Matron. That is something
42 that you might have learned, if you went to High School
43 Did you ~~learn any~~ study Latin? Do you understand
44 what I mean by enemata?
45 Daisy did not, but said she was prepared to lear

(8)

46 Her ignorance, however, didn't seem to displease
47 the matron
48 Are you strong and healthy, and have you always
49 been so?. Let me explain in order to save time,
50 that two of the applicants to-day had had
51 rheumatic fever and yet they only mentioned it as
52 an afterthought [while still at school which means
53 that if they were employed here they might ~~be~~
54 collapse and become a nuisance at any given
55 moment] [and an expense]
56 Ive always been strong & healthy, [Underneath   Matron
57 her put: on clothes, the costume and the inked [?]
58 straw hat, she felt ~~the~~ her ~~proper~~ physical pride
59 ~~of her twenty 17 years~~ collect & extend itself like
60 a cat in the sun
61 And your sight & hearing are perfect?
62 Yes, they're very good. [TEST here Matron to ask
63 her about something in sight not much in sight
64 bring out austerity of the room]   reading glasses
65 You notice that I wear ~~glasses~~ myself. [I need them
66 now, but as a probationer I did not need them]
67 I've never had ~~any~~ ~~glasses~~ spectacles
68 Have you any physical defects?
69 What kind of defects? Daisy asked in a low voice
70 Any that I can't see, Miss Saunders, at a ~~rapid~~
71 cursory glance. You may be marked or scarred.
72 Your spine may be crooked... Have you any tendency
73 to pulmonary complaint She looked up sharply. Do
74 you understand what I mean by 'pulmonary'? - Yes it
75 means to do with the lungs. - Pertaining to the lungs,
76 the Matron said. - ~~Chest troubles phthisis. we're~~
77 ~~not consumptive in my family~~ At the same time,
78 I don't mean a weakly habit of complaint &
79 ~~fancied~~ imaginary aches or fancied weariness. You
80 realise perhaps that a grown woman must expect
81 to spend one fourth of her ~~life~~ in actual pain?.-
82 I suppose that's true considering your stays always
83 hurt a bit, where the laces come   Daisy said.
84 [Real pain I am referring to]
85 To resume, have you ever been present at a death
86 or a birth? (Daisy shakes head.) Finally my dear.
87 (me my dear startled Daisy) why do you want to
88 be a hospital nurse? - I wasn't there when my
89 mother died, but I wish I had been.
90

Wilson Harris

Intuition, Myth, Imagination, Memory

The wanderings of the soul after death are pre-natal adventures; a journey by water, in a ship which is itself a Goddess, to the gates of re-birth. In Vao the newly dead man is believed to arrive before the entrance to a cave on the sea shore, where he encounters a terrible crab. In front of the cave mouth is a maze-like design called the Path. As the dead man approaches, the crab obliterates half of the design, and he has to restore it, or else be devoured. The Path is the same one that he has trodden many times in the ceremonial dances, and his knowledge of it proves him to be an initiate. After completing the design, he must tread the mazes to the threshold of the cave.

Norman O. Brown, *Love's Body*

I adopted the above passage as an epigraph to one of my novels called *Carnival* which appears as the first volume in *The Carnival Trilogy* (paperback re-issue, 1993). What I have sought to do in this article is to bring home, in some degree, I hope – by re-visiting *Carnival* (in an unfinished canvas of work encompassing many fictions) – an *activity* of the Imagination that may give some insight into *motivations* that have driven me to write across the years against 'the grain of fashion' (as one critic put it not too long ago in a review of *Resurrection At Sorrow Hill*).

Carnival was published for the first time in 1985. The other fictions in the *Trilogy* are *The Infinite Rehearsal* (1987) and *The Four Banks of the River of Space* (1990).

In an address which I gave in 1986, at the University of Warwick, I may have astonished the audience when I said that the epigraph was a revelation to me. It appeared to validate *Carnival*. I had not known of the myth it embodies throughout the re-visionary of writing *Carnival*.

The validation it offers is peculiar and strange and indeed the myth undergoes translation or transformation in *Carnival*. I mention this, at the beginning of this essay, as it brings into focus immediately the comedic gravity of the unconscious, that I hope

to pursue, and its eruption into faculties of the subconscious and
the conscious in the fiction-maker.

Let me say straightaway that the myth – as it evolves in
Carnival – has no bearing on any dogma or creed.

The dead return from the comedic unconscious – from the
depths of the obscure or unfinished *genesis* of the Imagination –
to motivate the fiction-maker into plumbing strategies of creation
that diverge from predatory habit or bias or intolerance
enshrined in investitures of tradition.

We are only too well aware of the hideous conflicts between
religions and cultures around the globe. Ethnic cleansings are fast
becoming a cliché in the language of the humanities (or is it in-
humanities?).

I tend – as an imaginative writer – to equate such conflicts and
polarisations with an addiction in the tribal family to closure or
frame or garment or investiture that a culture may seek to absolutize in its ritual vocations or performances.

Despite the ravages that such absolutes bring it seems curiously
natural that societies continue to pursue the reinforcement of a
form or a pattern that they may seek to impose on others. I put
it in this rather extreme way but the fact is, I think, that the reinforcement of self-interest in the vested body of a culture may
seem, as I have already implied, a natural ruling programme of
activity rooted in fate or necessity.

Yet the yoke of fate or necessity may evolve in the Imagination
into *the gravity of freedom....*

When the dead wear the investitures of culture or religion in
Carnival they are fiction. I repeat *they are fiction.* They are a
source of irony (as much as divine comedy) within the natural
assumptions and bodies of the obdurate living. They assist in con-
verting the living themselves into a malleable fiction in space and
time. They provide a species of evolution beyond the mind-set of
a grossly materialistic age. They occupy a seminal and changing
extremity within the yoke of fact. They imply uncanny gravity
and responsibility within the nature of freedom.

Freedom brings the license of adventure, it brings the power to
reach far afield, manipulate, strip others. Freedom seems at times
the invisible cornerstone of citadels of conquest.

Freedom, nevertheless, may make us aware of our own dire
predicament in the miring of living landscapes, in every ultimatum
that is extended into species in nature threatened by extinction.

Freedom's new intimacies, with the real threat of extinction in a nuclear age, brings us, I would suggest, upon a borderline between absolute investitures of tradition, that are narrow and fortressed, and divergence from these into a re-visionary dynamic. The threat of extinction overshadows the future as much as the past, unborn generations as much as the victims of polarised Mankind within past centuries whose silent lament remains. One may say then that the Imagination of freedom begins to acquire a new orchestration of pasts and futures in the returning dead. Their return brings an uncanny awesomeness into the womb of time....

Let me return to *Love's Body* from which the epigraph to *Carnival* comes.

In the Spring of 1983 I visited the University of California and conducted a series of seminars at the Santa Cruz campus. Norman O. Brown, the author of *Love's Body*, participated and at the end gave me a signed copy of his celebrated book. This remarkable study depicts a progression and a labyrinth of philosophies, religions, legends, myths, and is sustained by meticulous scholarship, analyses and summaries, allusions to sources and relevant texts.

The edition I was given appeared in 1966 but it was new to me. I returned to London after the seminar but did not begin reading the book until much later towards the end of the year. On a sudden impulse, on the completion of *Carnival*, I pulled *Love's Body* from a shelf – where it had reposed in peace – and began turning its pages at random to come upon the passage I underlined immediately for use as an epigraph to the fiction whose living typescript, it seemed, scattered on my desk, responded in my mind to the unforeseen choice I had made.

Here was a constellation or grouping of themes which I had pursued independently in the writing of *Carnival*. Those themes were not static. They had evolved and changed in all sorts of peculiar ways in the novel but they were recognisable. Perhaps I had known in childhood of the myth that the chapter embodied, but had forgotten.

I felt pretty sure this was not the case even if it were now incredible that my personal unconscious (in distinction from the Jungian collective unconscious) should store the nuclear body of the myth, in my voyaging imagination, across crowded decades: and that, as I shall show, the form that storage took, the way it released itself in *Carnival*, bore on a 'divine comedy of twentieth-

century existence' which I sought to bring into serial focus in
writing the novel. That intention is clear in the other epigraph that
I chose before I started *Carnival*. This epigraph – deliberately
chosen, even before I began, in contradistinction to the one which
claimed my attention at the end of the writing – comes from
Laurence Binyon's translation of Dante's *The Divine Comedy* and
runs as follows:

> His hand on mine, to uphold any falterings,
> ...
> He led me into the secret things.

The allusion, in these lines, is to Virgil, whom the great thirteenth-century poet invoked from the dead as his guide through
the *inferno* and the *purgatario*. Virgil is therefore, I would say, a
witness of the necessity for supreme fiction in divine comedy.

Dante's vision of space differed from ours. He saw the stars as
fixed. We see the stars as light-year shadows. We do not know
whether a star in the night-sky is actually extinct. It may have died
a million years ago but the news has not yet reached our eyes or
telescopes. Equally it may have been subject to a peculiar resurrection.... The visionary apparition, within light and shadow,
within the genesis of the Imagination (the genesis of apprehensive
sensibility in art and in science) remain curiously unfathomable in
the womb of space which we share with galaxies and beyond into
parallel universes.

Perhaps the fixed premises of space in the thirteenth-century
mind mirrored, in a sense, Christendom's yoke to necessity and
fate. Dante's genius lay in summoning pre-Christian Virgil as his
guide. But Christendom's closed investitures and rituals made it
inevitable, perhaps, that Virgil would be barred at the gates of the
paradiso. He would suffer the fate of an outcast.

In *Carnival* I raise the implicit question: was Virgil confirmed
as an extinct creature (despite his labours in the *inferno* and the
purgatorio) or may we pick him up and clothe him afresh in a re-
visionary dynamic within the twentieth century? Let me return to
the opening sentences in the epigraph to *Carnival* from *Love's
Body*.

> The wanderings of the soul after death are pre-natal adventures:
> a journey by water, in a ship which is itself a Goddess, to the
> gates of re-birth.

I was startled by these lines. Let me chart their correspondence in *Carnival*. Everyman Masters dies in London in the summer of 1982 and returns to Jonathan Weyl's dreams. *Masters is Weyl's Virgilian guide.* He secrets himself on a Wheel of the unconscious, subconscious, conscious and brings into play the revolving, sometimes precipitate, events of his life re-lived in Weyl's dreams. For instance, he discloses how he ran in a panic from a threatening figure on New Forest beach, South America.

> He ran into the town, found the gate to his house, up the steps....He entered and soon at the door to his mother's bedroom. He peered through a crack in the wood. His mother was seated at a table with a mirror. She was naked from the waist up and her breasts shone in the glass. She turned into a living vessel, half-glass, half-flesh. Everyman – a child of nine on this occasion – was precipitated into her body from the Wheel in his panic. He knew her panic. She was filled with fear. She contemplated aborting him. The year was 1917. Millions had died that year in war and other disasters....

Everyman is saved by the intervention of his mother's cuckolded husband who accepts the unborn child as his own, to be cared for in the future as his own.

If ever tribal nature – in its territorial imperatives and badges, its kith and kin ownership of flesh-and-blood, pigmentation clans, race clans – needed to be overturned by a brooding responsibility in the spiritualization of the Cuckold, then 1917 was an appropriate year for such overturn on the Wheel of Dream.

1917 was potentially a year of scandal and humiliation for Everyman's mother. It was a year which added to the tide of innumerable orphans around the globe within savage, continuing war.

No wonder the Cuckold was sometimes regarded in early Christian folklore as a dark saint or clown – in contradistinction to legends of rape – who gives shelter to outcasts from the institution of the orthodox family.

I mention 'legends of rape' in the paragraph above because Everyman's flight as a boy of nine was occasioned by a dreaded figure which loomed as a rapist on the beach of New Forest. He had been playing with a cousin called Thomas who had disappeared in a clump of bushes.

I won't attempt to go into the details associated with the flight except to say that they assume a curious staggered form on the

Wheel of Dream that Weyl experiences after Everyman's death in London.

Let me say also that an equation exists between the looming rapist and the legend of abortion as Everyman Masters sees himself precipitated backwards across the years of the twentieth century into the half-flesh, half-mirroring womb of space.

Carnival does not declare that Everyman's mother was raped.... But the ambiguities of intercourse between men and women, the wounds which women have endured – and which are reflected in a way on Everyman's body since time began – occupy the rhythms of carnival fictionality.

This is obviously a peculiar area of the novel. I would need to consult the drafts on which I was engaged in writing *Carnival* but I no longer have them. They were acquired by the Humanities Centre at the University of Texas at Austin. I may be able to illumine however how 'musicality' and 'masking' are active in the re-visionary process....

★   ★   ★

I was conscious of different levels of narrative – whether myth, divine comedy, novelistic pattern – reflecting diversities of approach to tradition. But equally these levels were linked – as if by a stranger hand in my writing faculties – by a rhythm *in which the wounds in the body of carnival fictionality – in the characters I portrayed in Carnival* – were so turned around and around that I was steeped in them at times as the genesis of humiliation and sorrow; at other times they became the *mystery of shape, the genesis of sculpture,* the 'unfinished stroke of genesis and creation', (*The Carnival Trilogy,* page 19).

No absolute pattern can disclose such numinous diversity in a blow or a wound except a rhythm for which there is no formula, a music that cannot be located or captured which is active nevertheless as upon the broken strings or chords of an invisible orchestra that may saturate, in some degree, the language one uses.

The boy Everyman Masters – in his game with his cousin Doubting Thomas – suffers a wound from a sharp bone on the foreshore of New Forest. He recalls legends of the golden man El Dorado who was sculpted, it was said, from the wood of a cherry tree.

Thomas bandages the wound, as if to prove its existence in the body of the Golden Man in the limbs of a child. The ghost of the Golden Man resides in the wounded child.

> I looked around for the axe that had cut the tree, as the bone had cut the spirit of childhood into light-year bandaged ghost, and thought I discerned it far out upon the retreating tide when a glimmer of sun upon a wave transfigured the ocean into lilting, sighing, singing sharpness. That was the shaman's axe! It was he (El Doradon shaman or space-priest) who had axed the tree a long time ago and sculpted from it El Dorado himself, El Dorado's retinue, his court, his wives, his children, his peers, his civil servants.
>
> All had come alive under the subtle liquid blow of the axe, and I recalled Pygmalion's ivory Galatea breathing all of a sudden under the chisel. So too had the wood, sliced from the cherry tree, turned to gold then to flesh and blood.
>
> Were axe and chisel and bone the same liquid tool across parallel light years? I seemed to see it all save that the shadow of uncertain voice or lilt of the cosmos, in all carven broken things, persisted....
>
> I felt divisions of sorrow within that blow, divisions of true shaman or creator and false shaman or manipulator of defeated cultures. I felt divisions of sorrow within a universal genius of love that seems at times in pawn to a universal seducer of humanity....
>
> I was at a loss to understand it all, though I had glimpsed again the transfigurative wound of which Masters spoke on so many occasions. He desisted from saying anything more at this stage though I knew now that his guidance into realms that seemed to exist before birth and after death bestowed upon me this life (this lived life) a privilege that would deepen and expand the biography of spirit on which I was engaged. It would deepen it, expand it, in peculiar and mutual engagement between author and character at the heart of Carnival.
>
> (*The Carnival Trilogy*, pages 18, 19 and 26)

The 'transfigurative wound' then – in the above passage – reflects a numinous centre an imaginative writer may entertain as the ground of supreme fiction. That centre – as I perceive it – involves us in the rhythm or music of constructive genesis, in a 'blow' or 'slicing' or 'shaping'....Yet another 'blow' – administered by the axe or chisel of the false shaman – apes genesis and subscribes to a pattern of, and fascination with, violence. One's apprehension of the 'centre' cannot be divorced, in all the circumstances, from 'divisions of sorrow'. At a certain level the two 'slicings' may appear the same blow or absolute slice. But they are not the same within a grave comedy that diverges from investitures of sameness that we may take for granted as the logic of realism or material-ism.... In such 'sameness' resides a proclivity to invest in patterns of universality that a dominant culture seeks to impose on others which are deemed inferior....

I need to move on now to 'a journey by water, in a ship which is itself a Goddess....' In unveiling his 'pre-natal adventures after death' Everyman Masters unveils not only the threat to his foetal existence in the year he was born but, implicitly, the plight of millions, the Abortion of an age (the waste, the terror), sprung from a civilisation involving men and women alike. Everyman's return from the dead is a re-visiting of past years upon a Wheel of Dream precipitated into Jonathan Weyl's book or 'biography of spirit'. Everyman wears many masks in *Carnival*. When he unveils the predicament of humanity in the womb of space – through the half-flesh, half-glass body of his mother – he is Weyl's Virgilian guide. Had not pre-Christian Virgil been rendered an outcast at the gates of the *paradiso*? Was not the *paradiso* compa-rable to the womb spirit in thirteenth-century Christendom? Weyl's 'biography of spirit' therefore is a quest for divergence from absolute closures in tradition that have bred savage conflicts. In such divergence the life of the 'transfigurative wound' is an essential ingredient in the body of freedom....

I mention this because anyone who has read Norman O. Brown's *Love's Body* would have noted a significant omission in the passage I quote from it which serves as an epigraph to *Carnival*. I omitted the gender of the 'terrible crab' as given in *Love's Body*. In the game that Everyman Masters and Doubting Thomas play on the foreshore of New Forest a crab appears on the Wheel of Dream to signify creation and creature, crab nebula and masquerades and constellations.

I knew nothing of *Love's Body*, as I have already said, when I wrote *Carnival*. Let me quote the passage I omitted from the epi-graph. It runs as follows:

> female monster...crab woman with immense claws, or a giant bivalvular mollusc, clam, which when opened resembles the female genital organ, and which shuts to devour.

None of this is applicable to *Carnival*. The 'crab' – it may be said – anticipated Everyman's unveiling of his mother's body, as mirrored in her bedroom, but if it is pertinent to any gender then it is to the looming male rapist or 'seducer of humanity'. But the truth is that the 'crab' – as it emerged in my fiction – is not placed within any absolute gender. It is a feature of 'masking' and 'musicality' within orchestrated technologies that may promote foodbearing regimes on earth, and in space, even as it is a medium of rocket warfare, tanks, cannon etc., etc. It is pertinent to the voyaging imagination. Its opacity lends itself to a contrasting comedy of fragility or transparency in all creatures subject to the violent tread of progressive machinery.

Everyman's 'glass' mother bears on the vessel in which Masters and Weyl voyage from South America to Europe in 1957.

1957 is the year of Sputnik and the technology of Sputnik is presented in *Carnival* as a symptom of the twentieth-century *inferno*. Masters unveils the ship to Weyl, on the Wheel of Dream, as a vessel of glass in a mighty storm. The womb of space now encloses them both and they look through its transparent walls on Christ walking on the huge waves, (*The Carnival Trilogy*, pages 85-88).

I would have liked to have quoted from the actual text than give the brief paraphrase above but the room for such a long passage does not exist in this article. So much anyway for a 'journey by water' through contrasting densities and transparencies that are linked by what I would call cellular rhythms in the chemistry of the prose.

One such cell brings home the pertinence of the 'ship which is itself a Goddess'.

I stress 'chemistry' and 'cells' as another aspect of 'masking' and 'musicality' through which we may perceive, I would suggest, *rehearsed links* between all vessels, however remote these may seem from each other.

All vessels are vulnerable and finite and to absolutize them is to bar the way to the conversion of extremities (associated with extinct or threatened species and cultures) into grave but paradoxically favourable conditions for the eruptive conscience of responsibility in arts of freedom and for the 'incubation of new forces, new energies' (*The Carnival Trilogy*, page 106).

Latent memory falls below daylight consciousness and it is the task of the Virgilian guide, an outcast into the womb of space, imbued with the force or energy of a preternatural eye, to lead his

protégé Weyl into a vision of his sick mother (Weyl's mother) as
a queen in a waterfall or upon an ocean, her body the mast of a
ship.

The two women, Jonathan Weyl's mother and Everyman
Master's mother, are victims of the malaise of a civilisation which
offers, nevertheless, a keen apprehension of the conversion of
extremity into transfigured being.

Jonathan Weyl, then, is a creature of latent memories and
trauma activated by Dream. His mother experienced a breakdown and post-natal illness after he was born. Out of latencies
then – latent memories erupting from the body of the unconscious – the apparition of a Goddess or a Queen places its mark
upon his mother and upon Everyman's mother.

> Queen Jennifer [Jonathan's mother] stepped out of a shower, out
> of a waterfall, out of an ocean, into the bedroom. I was lying half-
> asleep, half-awake, on her bed. She handcuffed me to her body
> as to the mast of a ship.
>
> (*The Carnival Trilogy*, page 91)

Jonathan sees himself handcuffed to the mast of a ship in, or
on, his mother's body....

His mother is described as a Queen. And this is as close as
Carnival arrives to a carnival Goddess in the epigraph to the novel
that I chose from *Love's Body*. Unmistakably, I would suggest, the
transfigurative linkages with Everyman Masters's mother can be
read in the rhythmic dimensionality of imageries – *mast, mother-
ing body, glass ship in a storm, half-glass, half-flesh mother* in which
Everyman experienced the peril of potential extinction.

The linkage of the two women is achieved, I would suggest,
through different narratives orchestrated, nevertheless, in a *rehearsal
of proportions*. No investiture or vessel or proportion is absolute.

The peculiar confirmation of the Goddess Ship was an aston-
ishment to me. At the time I did not know of the ancient myth in
Norman O. Brown's *Love's Body*. It is of interest to note that
'shower' becomes a 'waterfall' and an 'ocean' in the infant child's
eyes of Weyl, which the Virgilian guide opens to latent reality.
Time and space do not permit me to comment on Waterfall
Oracle or upon Amaryllis (Jonathan Weyl's beloved Beatrice) in
Carnival.

The orchestrated capacities of a mother-ship, and a bride-ship,
may be discerned in a close reading of all my fictions from *The*

Guyana Quartet (1960-63), through successive novels into *The Carnival Trilogy* (1985-1990), into *Resurrection at Sorrow Hill* (1993), into *Jonestown* (1996).

The term 'nove' means 'new' to me, within paradox and age, in its revelations of upper worlds and under worlds upon a Wheel of Dream....

Christopher Meredith

Telling and the Time

In a sense, how a book gets written doesn't matter. What matters is the fact that it does get written. What concerns me in the writing isn't so much the method as the murky thing in my mind that's asking to emerge. Concentrating on bringing that thing to the surface is such an effort that sometimes I'm hardly aware what methods I'm using. So for the sake of a piece of writing like this chapter, I look back over drafts and notes with a certain amount of surprise, not so much reminding myself what went on as discovering it. Sometimes the pain, effort, boredom etc. that I remember is borne out by the gratifyingly tortured look of the old pages. Sometimes there's a worrying lack of evidence of suffering. And occasionally my notes look disturbingly business-like and organised – I'm glad to say these moments are rare – like the calculations of some icy intelligence, though I know that at the time the whole thing was a bewildering muddle.

My first two novels were written in very different circumstances. The first, *Shifts*, a story about Welsh steelworkers in the seventies, was written when I was working full-time as a schoolteacher. It was written in spare moments and took almost four years to complete. There were seven years between my writing the first sentence and getting a copy of the book in my hand. A novel can be a large chunk out of your life.

Although I was beginning to get published as a poet and was contributing to magazines, writing *Shifts* was a fairly secretive process. I wasn't even entirely sure if it was a novel at first. It engaged me totally at certain times, but there were times when I wrote very little, when there were silences. How I persuaded myself to finish it is a little unusual. I published my first collection of poems at the end of 1984. Around that time I was writing little poetry, partly because of political conditions. The early eighties were particularly nasty. There was an atmosphere of political fear, with great erosions of civil liberties, the miners' strike, the Cardiff conspiracy trials. I addressed these things directly in a few poems, but found it difficult to continue with my other poetry. So with a book out and little else written I felt I had to work, but at what? I looked at the perhaps-novel which I'd started three years before and decided to make myself work on it every day of the week until it was finished. And that was how I completed a second draft of *Shifts* by the following summer. This may make it sound like a retreat from the real, but in fact it was the opposite, a movement broadening from the merely personal towards the larger processes of life.

By contrast the second novel, apart from being very different in style and on the face of it in content, came out of different circumstances. I realized that trying to write novels in my spare time was a likely route to an early death, so I decided I wouldn't write another unless I could make time to work on it properly. This was what I did. Although I'd made some notes for a new novel I did nothing about them for three years – by which time the publication of *Shifts* helped me get enough money together to write full time for about fifteen months, in which I finished a second collection of poems and wrote the bulk of the historical novel *Griffri*, the 'autobiography' of a Twelfth Century poet.

This time I actually had a desk to sit at rather than a corner of the kitchen table or the living-room floor or the public library of an evening. The process was now no longer secretive but public. My first two books were fairly successful critically, anyway, and people actually knew I was writing a new one, which exerted an unfamiliar pressure.

But although there were all these differences, the ways I worked on the two were comparable.

Both novels were written in their first drafts entirely in longhand. Most of my poetry, too, starts life in longhand, though typed drafts may come into the process a little later. I find working straight onto a keyboard useful when something's been commissioned, like this, and I'm pushed for time. I've also found working that way helpful on the odd occasion when I've tried to write a play. It's something to do with the speed at which I type and the speed of dialogue.

But for me, when it comes to prose I feel happier when I'm working with black ink on lined or squared creamy paper. I don't like looking at a screen. I like the quiet. I like the fact that I don't need an electricity supply. All I need is light, reasonable dryness, reasonable warmth, and a book and pen. At its simplest, writing satisfies the primitive drive to make things, and the satisfaction is all the more intense when the thing seems to be made, like a piece of music, out of air, out of almost nothing.

Writing *Shifts*, I got into the habit of dating each day's work. I find it handy to see how fast, or more accurately, how slowly I've been working to compare the time through which I've been experiencing the novel with the time it takes to read it. Rereading is important. I write slowly and allow a long gestation before I start, so I keep rereading to get an impression of how fast the piece will run past the eye of the reader. It's a bit like an animator making a cartoon where each frame has to be painstakingly drawn and then the lot run together to create an illusion of movement. I have to keep running the piece through the editing machine to make sure the pace is working the way I want it to. This kind of time is subjective, unlike the running-time an animator works with, and it depends on the skill and disposition of the reader as well as the author. To go back to the musical metaphor, the text is a score and the reader has an inner orchestra which performs the piece in reading.

For the second draft I go to the keyboard, but the really hard work has been done in that first longhand version. With both novels, and with the third, which I should be working on now instead of lounging around doing this, what I've found myself tending to do is to keep another set of notes as well as the draft itself. So there are the notebooks with the ongoing draft and nearby there are other bits of paper or a supplementary notebook where I'll jot down anything that occurs to me, sentences, sometimes whole passages which may come in later, or more general thoughts. I often write these notes in Welsh, as you see from some of the examples, especially when they're not specifically intended as actual bits of text. At the end of a day's work, if I'm lucky enough to have a sentence that might start the next day, I'll write that down in this extra notebook and avoid the pain of a start from cold. As the piece develops, these notes become more to do with structures, echoes, links, reflections involving the whole text.

Here are a couple of extracts from these supplementary notes:

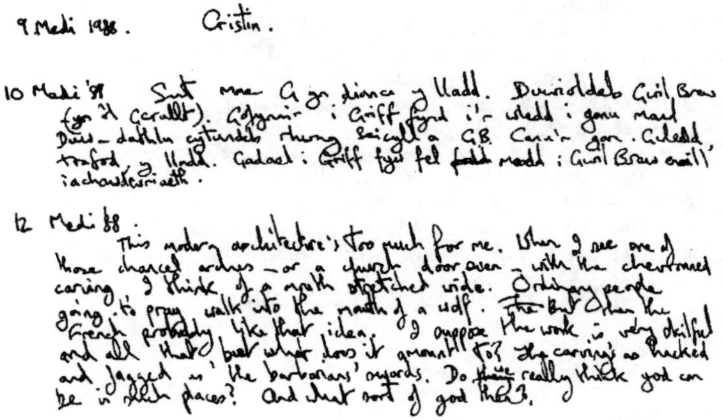
9 Medi 1988. Cristin.

10 Medi '88 Sut mae G yn dianc y lladd. Duwioldeb Gwil Braw (gyda'i Gerallt). Cyfryngwr: Griff fynd i'r wledd i ganu mawl Duw – dathlu cytundeb rhwng Seisyll a G.B. Canu'r gân. Cweryl, trafod, y lladd. Gadael: Griff fyw fel meddw; Gwil Braw ennill iachawdwriaeth.

12 Medi 88.

This modern architecture's too much for me. When I see one of those chancel arches – or a church door even – with the chevroned carving, I think of a mouth stretched wide. Ordinary people going to pray walk into the mouth of a wolf. But then the French probably like that idea. I suppose the work is very skilful and all that, but what does it amount to? The carving's as hacked and jagged as the barbarians' swords. Do really think god can be in such places? And what sort of god then?

1. Early notebook entries for *Griffri*

4 Mehefin 1985.   Pen. 7. tud 137.+.
      Chil drafen.
1. (137—141) ~~Ffatri~~ Oilatorman's cabin . Hagdahuke gyn diwmod
2. (141—143) Jack. Soaking Pits. Berw eira
3. (143—145) Keith.   Ty. Herod a Jack . Bore.
4. (145–48) Judth. Bore sadwrn . Jack . Thawoi
5. (148–153). Jack. Yn y dre
[6. *(153–154). Keith. Shifft nos. Reheating furnaces * Tom?
7. (154—157) O. Bore . Kelu yn sôn am guychio
8. *(157– 160.) Jack. Nosusyth. Judith yn gurdi'r teledu*
9. (160 —163). O. Dan y rolls? Kelu yn gwaelidd yn gadol
10. (163 —170). Keith. Nosusyth. Paratoi. Jack a Fred yn
        gwylio'r teledu.
11. (170—176) Jack. Cabin Ber. Noman ar asung.

1. 2. 3. 4. 5.   }   7 .

Torti 6?

    x x
7. 11. 9. 8. 6.   }   8 .

Rewrite
11. For nill
to go down.
n au al sgrifenu
dechrang
"The following day the
mill was closed."

7. 11 → nuints 8. 9. 10   }   8 .
                                              Gingerly
   ↓   ↓   the following night.
   ↓   V   ↓
 0   ↓   ↓   ↓
   ↓   Jack Keith O. Keith.
   ↓   ↓   ↓   ↓   ↓
Bore. y'm bore
ar noswith y naon Berg   Nosur gurlyned .

┌───┐
│ Pennod 7 . 1. (137–141)   │
│   2. (141–143)   │
│   3 .   │
│   4   │
│   5. (— 153) .   │
│ Pennod 8 newydd:7 (154–157).   9.(160—163)│
│   Dim atroidyg 11 (170–176) 10. (163—170).│
│   68   (157—160)   │
│   6. (153–4).   │
└───┘
  a'il Khifo'r pennodau o 8 ymlaen.

2. Late notebook entry during the redrafting of *Shifts*.

The first is three entries from notes on *Griffri*, made about a month before I started to draft the text itself. 'Medi' is Welsh for September. The first entry simply notes a possible name for a character. The second, in Welsh, is already trying to work out an aspect of an event likely to happen close to the end of the novel. The third entry, dated 12 September 1988, improvises a few sentences that might play a part. In fact they did influence some passages that appeared in Chapter 12 of the first part of the finished novel.

The second extract is from notes I made during the re-drafting of *Shifts* in June ('Mehefin') 1985. It's taken me a while to rediscover what the hell I was doing, but I realize now that these notes are an attempt to restructure what was Chapter Seven of the longhand draft into what became Chapters Seven and Eight of the novel. I've reread the section and noted its eleven parts, giving their page numbers in brackets followed by a brief note in Welsh of the content of each scene. Having drawn myself that map, I've tried to work out how to re-order the parts, considered cutting part Six ('torri' means cut), and in the place marked with arrows I've paid attention to how the way I'm contemplating reordering parts will affect switches in point of view and the chronology of the piece. The boxed section is a summary of the re-ordering which I can refer to when I'm typing the rewrite from the longhand manuscript. Finally I've made a note reminding myself to re-number the chapters from Eight on.

Phew. That's what I mean by the notes getting to be more to do with structure the further I am into the piece. But such major surgery has been fairly rare for me so far, though it suggests the growing complication of the process which otherwise creeps on invisibly. It's as though you can make the first mark on the canvas anywhere, but the second mark has to relate to the first, the third to the first two and each of them to the other two, and so on – so there's a sort of geometric progression in the complexities of composition. And of course it doesn't only apply to the way the paragraphs or sections are arranged, but to the control of tone, languages, image, symbol, and so on. Once you understand this process, the first sentence gets to be almost as hard to write as the thousandth, which is one of my numerous excuses for spending such a long time thinking before I start.

I find this leading to a question that's often asked, which is to what extent is the thing planned? Perhaps all my writing, and

especially large items like novels, is a combination of conscious
control and that murky thing, the given, that swims up at you, of
the aware bit at the front of the brain and whatever's going on at
the back somehow working together in an uncomfortable and
unstable tussle. So that in my case the answer to such a question
is that the piece can't be entirely planned because the process is
at least partly one of discovery.

It's very easy, during the thinking stage, to gloss over the tricky
bits, to say: well, there's a gradual change and so-and-so begins
to think such-and-such – the generalization is easy to make, but
it's extremely difficult to portray it incrementally happening, like
something real, so that rather than being just understood it's *felt*
in the reading. The novels are partly to do with such processes.
You may have an idea events may follow a certain course, but you
won't discover whether language and the material will let them
until you get there in the writing.

More specifically, in the case of *Shifts*, I had an idea of the
broad pattern, I even scribbled a few headings on the back of a
concert ticket early on, but the how and the who and the why
were mysterious to me.

Griffri was different in this respect because it's set eight centuries ago and based in part on real people and events – which
explains why I could be thinking in detail about moments near the
end of the novel before the real writing started. So a bit more
planning, and even some research was needed. It's also different
because the timescale is much longer, and this is a second aspect
of telling and the time which I want to touch on, that is the fictional time in which the story takes place.

The events in *Shifts* happen in about nine months; *Griffri* spans
forty years. The text is longer than *Shifts*, but not proportionate-
ly longer, so fictional time operates in peculiar ways. This can
have an effect on that other kind of time I've already mentioned,
pace, of course. I wanted *Shifts* to be slowburning, physical and
exact. I wanted a pacier, teasing sense of things happening quickly in much of *Griffri* so that often the narrator himself is confused.
I didn't want to be any more confused than usual myself, though,
so with an alien setting which had to be densely imagined, a bigger canvas, more characters and a much longer fictional time, I
had lots of problems of control and continuity. For instance, I was
aware that I had to be careful that the characters all aged at the
same speed so that they seemed to inhabit the same universe. To

help keep this in mind, I drew up rough charts with characters' names across the top, a list of events and dates underneath and then the ages of each of them at key moments in the grid this made. So I could look up the year 1171, for instance, and see the relative ages of the main people in the story. This little piece of machinery meant I wasn't constantly bothered by such details and could focus better on the serious stuff of the novel.

An irony of this is that no dates appear in the novel itself. We're never even told what century we're in. Since it's a first person narrative and the then conceptions of time were different from ours, Griffri, the speaker, would hardly keep telling us the date. He sometimes mentions people's rough ages, but actually he doesn't even know his own age exactly and mostly numbers don't matter. Even so, for me, the author standing behind the narrator, a firm idea of the structure in terms of our understanding of time is necessary for the story to work.

Like the way time and pace are handled, issues such as this concerning narrative technique may scarcely be given a thought by the casual reader, but they have to be got right for the thing to come off. And it's a mistake to think that first person writing is a simple or primitive form. In effect you have to shoot your entire film with just one camera, your narrator, and the character and complexities of that narrator are mercilessly exposed at great length, so that the invention and its execution must be particularly good if they're going to convince. Although in a way in *Griffri* I was setting myself arbitrary limits, like a poet trying to write a sonnet, to see what the limitations of the form would release, I can see that there were positive reasons for using first person. For instance, as Griffri's a man of his time talking to a contemporary I avoided having to do a lot of stagey medieval set dressing. Griffri doesn't have to tell us about all the lepers, one legged beggars covered in pustules, etc., all that stuff that makes a lot of 'historical' writing unbearably corny. He doesn't bother with all that just as we might not bother mentioning there's a carpet on the floor or a table in the room. More seriously, the novel came partly to be about memory, imagination, identity, and the narrative form is integral to those themes' development. Narrative form is woven into what the fiction can do and be about.

In the case of *Shifts,* the technique that emerged in the first chapter and then became the form for the whole book was one moving between, roughly, four points of view, mainly in the third person but sometimes slipping into or implicitly towards first person when it made sense for that to happen. What that meant was that the novel, in I hope a fairly unobtrusive way, had to have at least four different sets of imagery, at least four slightly different kinds of language, at least four styles. Then between those were connections, echoes, contrasts. I found I'd got a technique that allowed me to do all sorts of things – I could write the same scene several times over from different points of view, for instance. It was my first novel and there was a danger that I'd be like somebody's dad with a new camcorder who keeps zooming in and out and panning wildly. But I tried to work the form as unflashily as I could, so that the technique would do little to draw attention to itself.

So, it was both gratifying and irritating that so many people commented on the book's 'realism' when it appeared, or (much worse) 'gritty realism' – gratifying because I'd never come across any convincing fiction about my own part of the world and that was something I wanted to achieve; irritating because, having applied a label, some people seemed not to bother looking at what else was going on. Perhaps 'grittily realistic' is just genteel code for working class. Anyway, I thought the tags limited some readers' perceptions and expectations of the novel.

So far, a rediscovery of how and in what circumstances these two books were drafted has led me to consider the relationship between fiction and time and to touch on narrative technique. I'll finish by looking at some nuts and bolts of drafting in the opening few sentences of each novel as they appeared in first drafts as compared with the final versions. I don't intend to look for profundities, but to talk about how the pieces changed shape and why, and the contrast between the two.

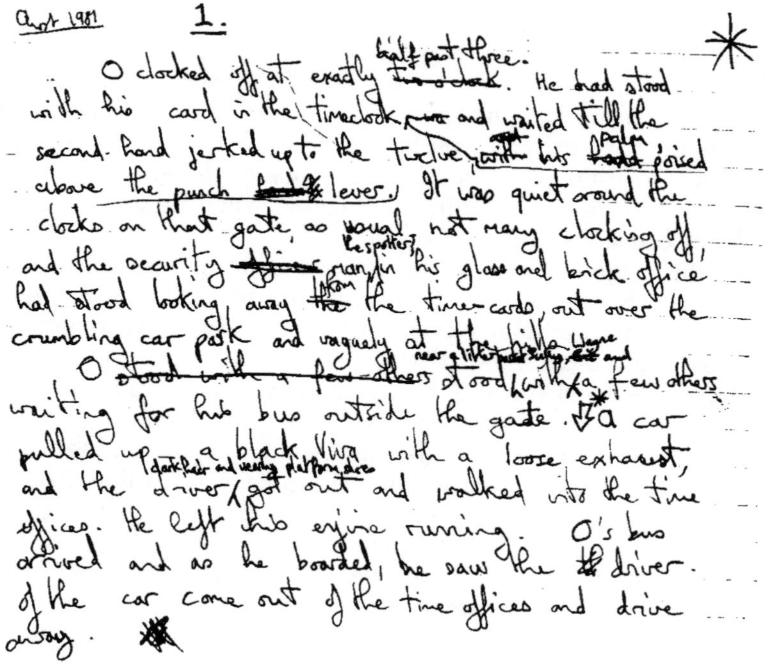

Aug 1981   **1.**

[handwritten draft:]

O clocked off at exactly ~~two o'clock~~ half past three. He had stood
with his card in the timeclock ~~~~ and waited till the
second hand jerked up to the twelve with his ~~~~ palm poised
above the punch ~~~~ lever. It was quiet around the
clocks on that gate as usual, not many clocking off
and the security ~~officer~~ *the spotter* man in his glass and brick office
had stood looking away ~~the~~ *from* the time-cards, out over the
crumbling car park and vaguely at ~~the hills~~ *near the litter basket with a few others and*
    O ~~stood with a few others stood~~ *[with] a few others*
waiting for his bus outside the gate. A car
pulled up, a black Viva *darkhaired and wearing platform shoes* with a loose exhaust,
and the driver got out and walked into the time
offices. He left his engine running. O's bus
arrived and as he boarded, he saw the ~~~~ driver
of the car come out of the time offices and drive
away.

ONE

O clocked off at exactly half past three. He had stood with his
card in the timeclock, his palm poised above the punchlever, and
waited till the second hand jerked up to the twelve. It was quiet
around the clocks on that gate, as usual, and the security man,
the spotter, in his glass and brick office, had stood looking away
from the timecard racks, out over the crumbling carparks and
vaguely at the hills.

O stood, as usual, near the litter basket with Sully, Wayne and
a few others waiting for their bus outside the gate. He looked
across at the bank of colourless grass and its few blackened,
unidentifiable trees. They looked dead but were only January
dead. In the spring, as always, they would put out just a few
leaves, only enough to show that somewhere in each of them
meagre life was continuing.

A car pulled up. A black Viva with a loose exhaust. The driver,
darkhaired and wearing platform shoes, got out and walked into
the time offices. He left his engine running. O's bus arrived and
as he boarded, he saw the darkhaired man come out of the time
offices, get in his car and drive away.

3. First draft and final version of the opening of *Shifts*.

The corrections made to the opening of the first draft of *Shifts* (3) are mostly minor. The crossings out and changes were made probably almost four years later after starting. I changed the clocking off time just to get the detail right. I rejigged the second sentence, starting 'He had stood', to make it more shapely. I inserted the Viva driver's dark hair because he reappears later and I wanted something by which he could be recognized. I added the platform shoes because by the mid eighties when I made the revision they'd become a period detail.

But the biggest change is the asterisk drawing attention to the arrow after the words 'outside the gate' in the second paragraph. You'll see from the final version that here I added two sentences describing half dead trees.

I liked the detail – it was based on some real pollution-blighted trees near the steelworks where I'd worked. It allowed me to introduce the time of year – January – and suggest through that longer, seasonal processes which in a quiet way simultaneously echo and contrast with the minutewatching time by which O lives. And there are other effects the detail has I resist exploring here.

But fundamentally, though it's been added to and I hope made richer, the feel of the extract hasn't changed from first to final draft. It looks as though I knew what I was after at the start, though I don't remember it feeling that way. It's a gentle beginning rather than a grand opening. There's the implicit but far from clear cut adoption of O's point of view. There's the unusualness of his name and the oddness of 'O clocked' with its similarity to 'o'clock'. There's a sense of things following an ordinary, miserable routine, with, in the final draft, the phrase 'as usual' recurring and echoed in the fractionally but significantly different 'as always' in the second sentence describing the trees. There's the absence of any sense of strong feeling or comment from O, which, because it's an absence, is likely to be undetected this early in a first reading. I think it's a risky opening, much riskier than a showy one. It's intentionally and perhaps off-puttingly low key, though this will change with a shift to another point of view in a few pages.

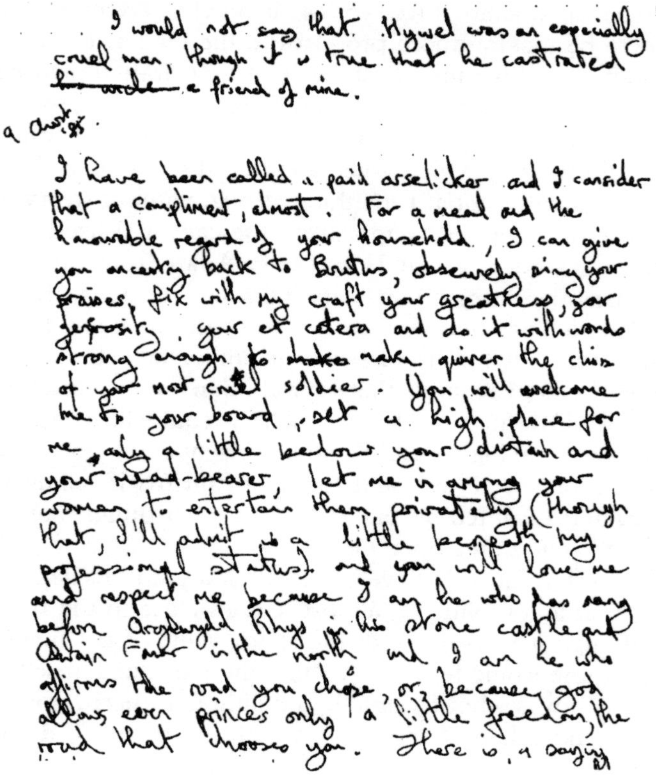

[handwritten draft notes]

I would not say that Hywel was an especially cruel man, though it is true that he castrated ~~his~~ ~~uncle~~ a friend of mine.

a chest ...

I have ~~been~~ called a paid arselicker and I consider that a compliment, almost. For a meal and the honorable regard of your household, I can give you ancestry back to Brutus, obscurely sing your praises, fix with my craft your greatness, your ~~generosity~~ your et cetera and do it with words strong enough to ~~make~~ make quiver the chin of your not cruel soldier. You will ~~welcome~~ me to your board, set a high place for me, ~~only~~ a little below your distain and your mead-bearer, let me in among your women to entertain them privately (though that, I'll admit is a little beyond my professional status) and you will love me and respect me because I am he who has sung before anybody Rhys in his stone castle at Certain Fort in the north and I am he who affirms the road you chose, or, because god allows even princes only a little freedom, the road that chooses you. There is a saying ...

1

Listen, Idnerth. I've been called a paid arselicker and I'm proud enough of my job to consider that a kind of compliment. After all, who with any sense would do such a thing if they weren't getting paid? For a meal and the high regard of your household I can give your ancestry back to Brutus, obscurely sing your praises, fix with my craft your greatness, your generosity, your et cetera, and do it with words strong enough to make quiver the chin of your most cruel soldier. You will welcome me to your feast, set a high place for me, only a little below your distain and your meadbearer, let me in among your women to entertain them privately — though that I'll admit is a little below my professional status — and you will love me and respect me because I am he who has sung before a dozen princes, who's not above telling the odd story as a lucrative hobble, who's sung to the teulu drawn in battle order, who is the keeper of memory, the lister of the dead, and I am he who affirms the road you choose, or, since god allows even princes only a little freedom, the road that chooses you.

(All right. So you're not a prince, I know. You Cistercians get so literal.)

4. First notes for and final version of the opening of *Griffri*.

By contrast the opening of *Griffri* (4) is much more of a firework.
It seems to be making more promises to the reader. I don't think
it is in fact, but it is much flashier. The first draft shown here is
a notebook jotting made years before I had a serious go a writing
the novel, before the period of gestation (and finding time) had
been lived through, which took another three years. The first
effort is just an attempt at something strong, without worrying yet
about those other marks to appear on the canvas. I liked the sentence 'I would not say that Hywel' etc. Apart from offering the
obvious narrative lure, it had black humour, tensions, themes of
cruelty and violence that were to develop with the book. But there
were problems. First, when I began to understand the shape the
novel might take, I realized that Hywel hadn't yet committed this
act when Griffri first speaks. I probably could have got round
that, though at a high cost. Second, this opening focussed too
much attention on Hywel, and too soon. Griffri is telling us his
own story and I wanted his talk to broach other things than would
have had to follow this opening.

My second go at it: 'I have been called a paid arselicker and I
consider that a compliment, almost' comes close to the final version. Although it loses some of the shock value of the first effort,
it has the same ironic tension. It shifts the narrator himself to the
centre, which was what I wanted, and although there's something
bombastic and self regarding in his manner, there's a disarming
and complicating element of self-deprecation even self-parody. I
was careful to use the word 'and' rather than 'but' after 'arselicker' so we hear the speaker trusting his listener to enjoy the
paradox without having it spelt out. In the final version, what was
the first sentence becomes the second. I've got rid of the dangling
modification 'almost'. The addition of the phrase 'proud enough
of my job seems casual and colloquial enough, but it brings in
notions of self-perception and self-worth and a lot of other significant baggage I don't intend to unpack here. Starting with
'Listen, Idnerth' feels immediate to me – a command rather than
a statement. I notice I've taken the word 'board' (for table) out of
the final version. I was probably originally thinking of the Welsh
word for table, *bwrdd*. But the English word is phonily archaic
and avoidable. 'Feast' is a mild archaism too, but isn't avoidable
for complicated reasons, and anyway it fits in more comfortably
with Griffri's deliberate coining of the language there. I brought
in the phrase 'lucrative hobble' so that a touch of self mockery is

present in the bathetic contrast of register between it and high-flown moments like 'I am he who has sung'. Another change is that I've cut the paragraph off after 'chooses you'. The paragraph now starts with an extremely short sentence and ends with an extremely long one. It blares the fact that it's first person and we know immediately the words are spoken – though that's a convention I'll be happy to shift from and to as it suits me. The strangeness of the name Idnerth perhaps gets us wondering where we are. There are several different kinds of language present, and a sense, I hope, of a self-conscious speaker, a performer deploying his skill with words and timing. His sentences lengthen as he warms up. Two of the first three sentences end on weak syllables, whereas the delayed final syllable of the last, long sentence is powerfully emphatic, and the question it touches on – the question of how much or how little we're in control of our own lives – while coloured by the complicating irony mentioned earlier, is both broached and emphasised. But the speaker undercuts his triumphant phrasing with the subsequent, apparently irritated aside in brackets.

As with any utterance, Griffri's talk bears both witting and unwitting testimony to his character, which isn't necessarily identical with the testimony it bears to the character of the author. As the paragraph's a half mocking attempt at self-description, the extent to which the testimony is witting is an intriguing question, and is related to the matter of the extent of control in our lives Griffri himself raises. But again, broadly I seem to have had some idea of what this book was to be like even at the outset, enough to reject a seductive but slightly off-target opening sentence quite quickly. It seems to have been a matter partly of waiting and watching and thinking the thing into focus and then sharpening it more in the work on the page.

Looking back over what I've said, I realize I've used a lot of visual metaphors – canvases, cartoon, video, film. Perhaps I have a fairly visual imagination, but it would be a mistake to conclude I think of the novel in cinematic terms. They're different forms. The textures of language itself are the substance of the novel in a way they just can't be for film. So I adopted the metaphors not in a profound way but as a pragmatic means of explanation.

All of this just scratches the surface. I think the discussion of the drafts shows that the whole chapter could have been built on considering the handling of language – register, diction, rhythm, and so on, so the metaphor would be the novel as big poem, though there'd be a danger that in the mass of detail we'd lose sight of fiction itself and the impulse towards imaginative unity.

For me, so far, writing novels has meant making these big, unified things, kinds of worlds – however supposedly realist the work may be – which cohere and are somehow consistent. Getting pace, fictional time, narrative form, the language right are all part of that worldmaking. That involves a lot of artifice, whether the writer's conscious of it or not. Often we may be unaware of the devices of our own work because they're culturally given and so taken as natural, become as invisible as *Griffri's* lepers or our tables and carpets.

If some of this chapter has made the business sound a bit cold and mechanical, it isn't. Of course you need practical skills and a certain cultural context. Writing a novel for me is the use of those skills, that shaping, on the emergence of the given stuff, the cussed, bulky, strange material that asks you to write it. Doing that is infinitely more engaging, though harder and paradoxically more real, than the wearying kind of writing I'm going to stop doing – now.

Jennifer Johnston

There Are Easier Ways of Earning a Crust, But This Is the One I'm Stuck With

I have recently finished my tenth novel. I find this quite aston-ishing, as back in 1969, or whenever it was that I finished my first one, I felt I had possibly about three novels in me; three pieces of work that were queueing up in my head to be given their free-dom and that, I presumed, at that faraway time, would be that. Thoughts and ideas, though, beget other thoughts and ideas; the queue in my head lengthened, queue-jumpers shoved and pushed, the feeble were left to wait at the back of the queue, while plays, monologues, characters, notions, dreams and fantasies that I never thought existed in my mind scrambled to the front. Sometimes the feeble would gain strength in the waiting, sometimes they would just shrug and go away.

If the above gives the feeling that I have very little control over what I write, that would indeed be true; to carry on the analogy of the queue, I am the bus into which these ideas climb and when we all reach our destination they get off and go their ways out into the world. The bus is then empty and ready for its next passengers.

I came to writing in a disorderly fashion at the age of thirty-five. I was married, I had children, I was living a pretty good life in London, doing the things I liked doing, seeing the people I liked seeing, but for several years a voice in my head had been insistently saying, 'This won't do you know. You have to do something with your one and only life. Hanging in there is not good enough.' Except of course that expression had not then been invented; I use it now because it amuses me to do so.

I have never yet worked out whether it was the voice of a good angel reminding me, somewhat magisterially, that I owed the world some effort, or a bad angel screeching, 'Get noticed, don't allow yourself to slip through life without being noticed.' I don't suppose it matters very much which it was. The persistence with which it spoke made me eventually move.

Even then when I started first of all to write I never enjoyed it.

It was dogged no-surrenderism that made me sit there day after day, writing, re-writing and then, over-critical and over-anxious, tearing up page after page in despair. It seemed quite a ludicrous way to suddenly start spending my days.

It was the day that I realised that I must finish a piece of work before bringing the critical side of my brain into play, that I first began to be a writer.

I was then starting to learn from my own mistakes.

Lesson number one: nothing is real until it is finished.

It is impossible to judge the weights and measures of a piece of work until the pattern has been established and the last full stop is in place. Then you have something to work with, to mould, cut and carve.

Let me give you an example of the sort of odd thing that happens when I start the writing process first on a new book: when I began tentatively to get *The Invisible Worm*, book number nine, down on paper, I had quite clearly two women in my head. One, a Dublin woman, who walked briskly each day on Dunlaoghaire pier, hail, rain or snow and talked to herself, made jokes to herself, was in fact healthy in her head; the other, Laura, who lived in the country and waited and wished for darkness to envelope her. At that time I was not quite sure why she had this strong desire and whether it was for death or the peace of madness.

I had the notion that these two women would meet and that out of that interaction the book would grow.

Instead, after a few weeks of writing, Laura took up more and more space. Her story, she insisted, was the one that had to be told. She demanded that I search out her secret. No meeting, no interacting was necessary. So the Dublin woman got shoved to one side; I gave her no more thought. She was, I thought, erased from my life.

Luckily, though, she was only biding her time in the shadows of my mind, because as soon as *The Invisible Worm* was out in the world, she moved inexorably to the front of the queue and refused to go away until her story also was told.

I was grateful for her reappearance as the nightmare of emptiness is always close to the mind of all writers. It is a terrifying notion to feel that you have typed the last sentence, put the last full stop on the last page, typed 'THE END' for the last time.

The woman, by this time called Stella, (a ghastly name, and it wasn't until I was well into the book that I realised why she carried it) trailed with her a whole lot of thoughts about love, lies, betrayal, secrets, power, marriage, mothers and daughters; also magic and the strange quirks of fate that make writers discover themselves.

I was also having daytime dreams of this man/angel hovering above me, his huge wings shimmering in some kind of light. For a long time I couldn't work out why he was bothering me so in the hope of some sort of exorcism I wrote out a description of the vision that was in my head and having pinned him to the page I found that he became the centrepiece of Stella's story.

It took me a long and wearisome time to write *The Illusionist*.

In fact, having written about thirty-five pages, I lost all energy and interest in it. I shoved all my papers away and instead concentrated on other things: I adapted one of my books for the stage, I wrote a film script and a couple of short plays, until one day my daughter-in-law said to me, 'Why are you trying so hard not to write your novel?'

Cheeky lady, I thought, but after a day or two I became filled with intolerable guilt, rather as if I were killing someone by inattention, so I got my papers out and began to re-acquaint myself with my characters and their lives. I tried to find out why I had wanted to write the book in the first place, tried to hear once more Stella's voice. It took a long time.

I had to edge myself back into the book, line by line; some days I wrote no more than a sentence, some days I sat in rage staring at a blank screen. I resisted the temptation to work on anything else and gradually I began to understand what I had been writing about; I began to feel the return of energy and confidence. It was almost like recovering from an illness.

The book is written both in the past-recollective tense and in the present-reflective tense. Each section is written in Stella's voice. This basically means that the time span for the book is twenty-four hours and also, at the same time, part of a lifetime. This seemed to me to be the easiest way in which to tell seamlessly the parts of Stella's story that I felt I wanted to tell.

I never write in chapters; this means that I have to find some other method of punctuation. It is therefore in *The Illusionist* the movement backward and forward in time that acts as punctuation.

Maybe to the reader this will seem a little arbitrary, but I hope not. I hope each move has its sense both in time and also in the general rhythm and thrust of the book. If there is a fault in this particular book, it is maybe that it floats in a somewhat abstract way along the side of society, of the reality of life.

I hope this doesn't diminish the work in any way as I set out, as I say in the early stages of the book, to examine a sliver of a life and to make some sense of the trailing thoughts that came along with Stella.

I prefer always to leave things unsaid, making the whole process of writing and reading a dialogue, rather than a lecture. I think a lot of readers are bothered by this, preferring to be told how to react to situations, rather than to join in the joyful exercise of creative reading.

I loathe the notion of the writer as some authoritarian figure. The reader must be given freedom to range at will within the laid perimeters of each writer's work.

When I started first to write *The Illusionist* I saw the opening section as the first scene of a play: indeed I wrote it as such. I wrote stage directions and all, setting the scene and then a couple of pages of quite good wry and energetic dialogue.

I then moved on to explain why I had started a novel in such an untraditional way. People who are not involved in theatre believe that they will find plays difficult to read; a challenge they don't want to accept. So, after the dialogue came to an end I wrote as follows:

> I would like to flesh out this room in which I sit; you see when you write a play you have to leave space for the director, the designer, the actors. They too have their place in that act of corporate creation, each of them in their own way enlivens, transforms the words on the page into an illusion of reality. For the reader you must be more specific, no point in saying... a room full of light and shade. Two long windows. That won't do at all. The reader needs to move, breathe in that room, smell the smokey scent of the newly lit fire which spits sparks from time to time onto a hearth rug all ready freckled with tiny burns.

I realised after I had returned to work on the book that this, though in its own way quite good, intelligent writing, and the dialogue and stage directions that had gone before it, had to go. It was giving out the wrong signals; it was creating a mode that I might find myself having to use later in the book, and as I moved back in with my characters I realised that this would be inappropriate, so I plunged straight in, beginning as I meant to go on, speaking with the voice of my heroine if that is what she might be called.

> I sit in a room full of light and shade.
> I dream.
> I dream of her entrance.
> She will come into the room as if she were coming onto a stage, or anyway that's the way I see it from where I sit, from where I think about it.
> A fire burns in the grate. From time to time it spits sparks onto the hearth rug and I make a mental note to chastise the man with the horse and cart from whom I bought the neatly chopped logs of wood, when next I see him.
> There are trees outside the window, just coming into leaf and the light in the room is filtered through the acid green of newly born leaves. A bright cold light.
> I imagine she will be dressed in black.

This is neater, more appropriate to the tenor of the book.

You can get yourself mightily snarled up by trying to be too clever!

Having said that I also have to say that writing is all about tricks and trickery, sleight of hand, illusion. Never be afraid of using tricks, just don't make them so obvious that the reader feels overwhelmed. The art of trickery is subtlety... now you see it, now you don't.

Here a few notions of advice spring to mind, though I don't suppose I have much to offer by way of advice that you don't already know.

Read...

That is the great imperative for any writer and shouldn't really have to be said, as I presume that all writers are readers. I don't otherwise know how you would come to that gate that has 'I have to be a writer' written on it, let alone push it open and go through.

Reading gives you the courage, because the more you read the more you realise the risks that writers take and you understand that if you are idiot enough to want to be a writer, you are also idiot enough to take the risks involved. Jump without the safety net... it's not easy, but it has been done before.

Think carefully of the importance of the first ten pages of your work. This is when you have to trap your reader. This moment is when you have to catch the reader's interest. This moment is when you have to intrigue, amuse, seduce, whatever it may be you wish to do, this is when it must happen. I would hate to admit the number of books I have thrown aside, never to pick up again, because I have not tasted the magic in the first ten... or perhaps I should say twenty pages.

Here, just for your delectation, are three openings that captured me instantly:

> On the day they were going to kill him, Santiago Nasar got up at five thirty in the morning to wait for the boat the bishop was coming on. (Gabriel Garcia Marquez)

> Stately, plump Buck Mulligan came from the stairhead, bearing a bowl of lather on which a mirror and a razor lay crossed. A yellow dressing gown, ungirdled, was sustained gently behind him by the mild morning air. (James Joyce)

> I have been in love with Evelyn Cotton for twenty-four years and four months less eight days. We have made love twice. The first time was twenty three years ago. The second time was yesterday. Does that make this a sad story: make me a comic figure? (Frank Ronan)

No fireworks, just good confident writing and the promise of pleasure to come and probably mysteries. I love mysteries. Perhaps that's really why I write.

Remember that every character, no matter how small, has to have the possibility of real life. When you first start to write you tend to use the minor characters rather like bits of furniture, or props in a play, but they too have to have the reality of the major characters. The reader doesn't have to know their life histories, but has to believe in their humanness. If you don't believe in the humanness of your subsidiary characters neither will your reader.

Writing is trickery. Never forget this.

The better the writer, the less visible the tricks, but they are nonetheless there. Even the shaping of a piece of work is trickery. To be an artist is to be an illusionist, a weaver of spells....

Read what you write out aloud to yourself.

Phrases, sentences, paragraphs have to sound right as well as make sense. Even abrupt and unsettling prose has its rhythms, and those rhythms help to give substance and an atmospheric sense to what you write.

I really can only tell you about how I feel, about my attitudes to the way I work and as you may have gathered from what I have written above I am a writer who does not enjoy writing. I like the notion of being a writer, but not the practice of writing. This is not to say that there are not moments when I look at a piece of my work and say to myself 'Yes. That is precisely right.' But by and large I find the whole process quite painful, but compulsive.

I see no other way of living my life. What else is there to say?

Caryl Phillips
Through the Fire

1. Why I write fiction (although strictly speaking this is not relevant to the subject at hand)

In her essay 'Professions for Women' (1931), Virginia Woolf talks about the necessity of killing what she terms 'the Angel in the House' before a woman can begin to write. She describes the soon-to-be murdered 'Angel' in the following manner. 'She was intensely sympathetic. She was immensely charming. She was utterly unselfish. She excelled in the difficult arts of family life. She sacrificed herself daily.' Eventually Virginia Woolf defeats 'the angel', although she confesses that 'she died hard', partly because 'she was always creeping back when I thought I had despatched her."

It seems to me that every writer has to begin by slaying a phantom of some kind. In my case I had to struggle with a phantom named 'Caution'. When, aged twenty-one, I finally declared that I wanted to be a writer, I was made aware of a number of facts. First, I was an immigrant. Second, I was a graduate of an important university. Third, I was the eldest of four. In other words, I had to be grateful for whatever success had already come my way, and I had to set a good example for those who would follow. I was expected to be cautious. However, it is impossible to embark 'cautiously' upon the journey of becoming a writer. Immigrant, graduate, eldest son; it mattered little to me how others wished to define me, for I had every intention of kicking 'Caution' into touch and getting on with the business of becoming a writer.

Why do I write? This is a question with which I am familiar. The subject at hand, however, is how do I write. This is a far trickier question and one which I will come to in a moment. But first, why do I write? Having dealt with the phantom of 'Caution', I found this question being put to me in a variety of different forms by, among others, journalists, bank managers, and anxious girlfriends. Why? What's the point? Mercifully, somebody else had already produced the perfect answer. George Orwell identified 'four great motives': Sheer egoism, aesthetic enthusiasm, historical impulse, and political purpose. He also suggested the following:

> All writers are vain, selfish and lazy, and at the very bottom of their motives there lies a mystery. Writing a book is a horrible, exhausting struggle, like a long bout of some painful illness. One would never undertake such a thing if one were not driven on by some demon whom one can neither resist nor understand. For all one knows that demon is simply the same instinct that makes a baby squall for attention.

He might well be right. But enough of this. The subject before us is, 'How do I write?' As I suggested, a far trickier question.

2. On breaching the security system

Where to begin? Most of the time the last thing I need is an 'idea' for a novel. Usually I am already working on a project, and if another idea begins to scale the security fence that I've constructed around my present task, and demands to be taken seriously, I regard it as an unwelcome intrusion. Sadly, from time to time, the security system will be breached and on such occasions, irrespective of what I may currently be dealing with, I have to pay attention.

It may simply be a phrase that enters my mind, and for some reason the phrase begins to suggest a book. This happened in the case of my first novel, *The Final Passage*. The notion of 'the middle passage', the journey on the slave ships which took countless millions from Africa across the Atlantic to the Americas had, understandably enough, always haunted me. Twentieth-century migration from the Caribbean to Britain involved a reverse crossing of the wide expanse of the Atlantic, and this seemed to me to suggest a 'final passage' of some kind. This phrase became lodged in the forefront of my mind and it refused to retreat to some convenient corner.

On other occasions I have 'found' the idea for a book while rummaging around in the library. This happened to me in the case of the novel *Cambridge*. I was sitting in the British Library when I decided to look up eighteenth and nineteenth century references to St. Kitts, in the hope that I might unearth some material which would enable me to unravel the mystery surrounding the history of an old plantation house on the island. Eventually I did find references to this now abandoned house which, as it turned out, had been famous in its day for its opulence and splendour. I realised that I wanted to embark upon the task of reconstructing the proud colonial history of this house which was once known throughout the Caribbean islands as a place of unparalleled grandeur.

With both *The Final Passage* and *Cambridge*, the idea for the novels interrupted other work that I was engaged upon. However, I did not stop working on my other projects, I simply logged the fact that an idea had shown up and it would eventually have to be dealt with. In the case of *The Nature of Blood*, I *did* stop working on my other projects for a few weeks. This was due in part to the strange manner in which the idea presented itself. One day I suddenly found myself writing down the following words, with no understanding of where they were coming from. In this case, the security system was not so much breached, as disengaged, dismantled, and packed away for a while.

Between us a sheet-thin gauze of fire that a sudden gust might
extinguish. But there is no wind. In the distance the low grinding
of a river as it slithers across smooth, warm stones. Night sits easily
on our shoulders. The scene is familiar.
Why you insist on speaking with me, I do not know.
Through the fire
Why you seem prepared to trust me with your story, I do not know.
Through the fire
As ever you stand before me, your eyes bright, your arms outstretched, your
palms upturned. You watch me. I imagine you have been with me my
whole life. Watching. And waiting.
Through the fire
Many years have passed since I first discovered you. You
troubled me then. You trouble me now. But mortality, like thunder,
rumbles its dull way toward me.
It is I who must take the step.
Through the fire
And come unto you.

3. Are you going to read all those books, or what?

Having stumbled across an idea (soon to become an obsession) which I intuitively feel will become a novel, I then begin to think seriously about how I might further acquaint myself with the subject. This involves the word, research. For instance, in the case of

The Nature of Blood, I was reasonably sure that the novel was going to be principally concerned with the Holocaust, but armed only with a general knowledge of the subject I felt that I had to become better acquainted with the history. This proved to be no easy task for the number of books, films, and other material on this subject is quite overwhelming. For some reason I decided to catalogue just how many books and films I read and watched during the three year period during which I was 'researching'. It transpired that I read or consulted one hundred and eighty books, watched fifteen documentary films, three feature films, and visited the Holocaust Museums in both Washington D.C., and Jerusalem. In retrospect I am not sure that all of this research was strictly necessary, but at the time it felt as though it was a process that I had to pass through.

Research is for me deeply tied up with two things. First, and most obvious, a desire to immerse myself in the subject-matter in order that the imaginative act that is to come might be more substantially grounded in 'fact'. This seems to me very important when one is dealing with 'sensitive' material such as the Holocaust, or the African slave trade. There is a great desire on my part to simply get it as 'right' as possible. Not only for reasons of factual accuracy, but I know that there exists a group of people known as 'revisionist' historians who would seek to convince the world that such events either did not happen, or if they did happen the 'facts' as we know them have been greatly exaggerated.

Second, and just as important, the act of research also involves my remaining alert to the possibility that some character, or characters, will emerge out of the welter of research, and present themselves as the people who will eventually 'drive' the narrative. I am not a novelist in the post-modern tradition who makes himself visible to the reader and orchestrates the narrative from the centre of the stage. I like to hide in the wings and turn the stage over to my characters. An occasional whispered prompt is all that I pemit myself. Therefore, without characters all I have is an idea and an ever-growing pile of 'research'. I cannot build a novel out of this flimsy material. I need people. And patience.

4. Weirdos, wackos, and other uninvited guests who show up to the party

Yo, there's a party going on! But either no folks, or the wrong

folks have shown up. The party is in trouble. Having recognised
the problem the anxiety-racked writer will naturally enough ask
himself, when are the right people going to show up? The answer,
my friend, is blowing in the wind. Who knows? I spend much of
my time in this 'gestation' period reassuring myself that I have the
right music, the right drinks, the right food, and eventually everything will be fine. But when? When? Meanwhile, I simply wait for
the uninvited guests to leave and the real characters to show
themselves. Thomas Mann's hero was peering at these self-same
welcome, but elusive, characters when, in the short novel *Tonio
Kroger*, he observed the following:

> As I write, the sea whispers to me and I close my eyes. I am look-
> ing into a world unborn and formless, that needs to be ordered
> and shaped; I see into a whirl of shadows of human figures who
> beckon me to weave spells to redeem them: tragic and laughable
> figures and some that are both together – and to these I am drawn.

The problem is, of course, that the writer may find himself
drawn to certain characters and, like Thomas Mann, he may even
be able to see them as shadows; but will they show up to the
party, sit down, and take part? Or will the uninvited guests continue to dominate the scene?

It is the quality of the guest list which largely distinguishes literary fiction from pulp fiction. Two-dimensional, flat, characters
– a type that we know from situation comedies, romances, and
thrillers – are easy to locate. Writers who utilise such people are
generally able to produce at a prodigious rate, for everybody who
turns up to their party is invited to sit down and put on a funny
hat. The literary novelist has to learn to distinguish between the
important guest and the gate-crasher. This is no easy task, and for
young writers eager to get their careers off to a flying start, the
cultivation of patience and the exercising of vigililance causes
them no end of heartache and frustration.

5. *How long will you be staying with us, sir?*

Perhaps I have spent too long working on films and television
scripts, but I always find myself describing the next two stages as
pre-production and production. Pre-production lasts anywhere
from four to eight weeks, and involves sorting out my files, re-
ordering the research, writing whenever the mood takes me, and

trying out the narrative voice or voices. This stage begins only when I am sure that I have located my characters, and it ends when I am 'pregnant'. In other words, when I cannot hang on any longer and I have to start writing in earnest. At this point – the onset of production – I invariably have to go away somewhere.

I like to write in hotels. I love the control that I have over the space. The 'Do not Disturb' sign that I can hang up whenever I please. The towels in the bathroom that are replaced every day. Somebody to come in and change the bed linen and make up the bed. The phone that I can pick up and order food or drink. The television that is there if I want it. Outside is the city, preferably one that I'm already somewhat familiar with. A city that I can step into and go for a walk, or go to the movies, safe in the knowledge that I am unlikely to see anybody that I know. Then back to the hotel. If I want to work through the night I can. Or, time-zones being what they are, I can simply call whoever I please in some far-flung part of the globe and say 'Hi, how are you doing?'. Or alternatively, I can just ignore everybody and get on with whatever I am doing. Nobody knows where I am. Nobody can get hold of me.

I usually last about two to four weeks in a hotel, then I go back 'home' for a few weeks. Time to answer mail, sort out my life, catch up with what ever has been going on in my absence. It is true to say that I generally also need a break from the work. Eight to ten hours a day, seven days a week, is a lot of writing and re-writing. A lot of concentration. However, after some time at 'home', I will once more leave, this time for a different hotel, in a different city, in a different country. And the process repeats itself. Two, three times. Maybe more.

Production lasts, for me, about six months. This may seem like a short time, but research, gestation, and pre-production, have taken anything from two to three years. The final six months is the hardest period, but if the rest of the work has been carried out properly, it is the most rewarding. The foundations of research have been established, I am sure about the characters, and they are now surprising me and twisting and turning the plot in unexpected directions. When I start to replace punctuation that only an hour previously I had removed, then I know that I am closing in on the end. And when I finally realize that I am mentally and physically too exhausted to improve the manuscript any further, then that is the end.

6. Still kicking 'Caution' into touch or How I've started to get fancy in my middle years

a) Computers: I came to these things relatively late. I wrote my first three novels in long hand and typed them up on a manual typewriter. In 1990 I paid a secretary to put the the final drafts of my fourth novel *Cambridge* onto something called a disc. This turned out to be a smart move because it meant that I could make all the minor changes quickly and not have to bother with typing the whole thing up again. After the experience with *Cambridge*, I now detected some virtue in this computer-gadget and so I decided that I should learn how to use one. I didn't. I engaged a research assistant for my next novel, *Crossing the River* and she certainly knew about computers. My ignorance of, and admiration for, the gadget continued until 1993. It was only after the publication of *Crossing the River* that I bought a laptop, and enrolled in a computer course at a community college in Massachusetts. I had arrived: I was computer-literate, although I still write long-hand and then transfer it onto the disc, hard or otherwise.

b) Assistants: To start with I did everything. I was broke, I had no choice. But then as the research started to get a little more complex I realised that I could save both time and energy if I put my hand in my pocket. Having somebody trustworthy to delve in libraries, deal with the intricacies of inter-library loan, do xeroxing, and find answers to questions of a factual nature is a blessing that I am grateful for. It is true to say that I could do most of it myself, but if I find myself sitting in a hotel room on the other side of the world, and I need some information immediately, it helps to have a capable and efficient person at the end of a phone. Also, writing is a lonely enough job as it is, and I confess to liking the teamwork involved in working with somebody else.

c) Hotels: To start with I would stay anywhere. In fact, during the writing of *The Final Passage* I slept in a rented Renault hatchback on a variety of beaches in Tenerife. I simply did not have the money for both a rental car and a hotel. Eventually I traded in the car for a desk and a bed, and I finished the novel in a Spanish 'flea-pit' that was masquerading as a hotel. A decade or so later I wrote *The Nature of Blood* while staying at more comfortable hotels in Toronto, Bangkok, and Amsterdam. I now work on the basis that the fancier the hotel the quicker I will write.

After all, the hotel bills will arrive before the advance for the book. I have to keep the gap between the two as short as possible. Twice I have turned up at hotels which have been perfectly acceptable, but I have shown up with only ideas and a little research, but no characters. Once in Spain in 1988 and once again in Cuba in 1993. I subsequently learned that hotels are zones for production not gestation. They are too expensive for mere head-scratching.

7. *Waiting for a Bus*

You see, in the end it all boils down to this. Trying to write a novel is like waiting for a bus in the rain. A number of buses appear and pull up at the stop, but you have to know which is the one that you should climb aboard. In other words, which is the one that contains the necessary idea that will become an obsession. Once on board there is more waiting. A little anxiety as you flick open your research texts and begin to read and gather material. A little worry about paying for the ticket. Concern about how long this journey is going to take. Yet more anxiety as you look around at the other passengers and begin to wonder which one of them (if any) is 'it'; a viable character. Finally somebody gets on board the bus and your eyes meet. You recognise the person and they recognise you. You gather up your texts and you stand before the person. They too stand, and one of you reaches up and sounds the bell. Together you step from the bus, and the two of you find yourselves alone on the pavement. You are clutching your research materials. You watch the bus trundle away into the distance and around the corner. You were on the right bus. You did your research. You waited patiently for the right character to appear. Now, as the bus passes out of sight, you are ready. But it is still raining.

Maureen Duffy

Write On

I began writing when I was about six and, in those immediately pre-Second World War days, it was in verse, rhymed and owing much to Robert Louis Stevenson. Why I began writing poetry I don't know. No one else in our family had, as far as we can remember, ever done such a thing before. My great-grandparents on my mother's side had been the first of her Essex forebears to be able to sign their own names since the family had sunk into virtual pauperdom, with much of the rest of the country, in the eighteenth century. Armed with their new skill my great-grandparents had left the impoverished village they had been born in and headed down the line to the great railway works in Stratford East where he found a job as a blacksmith. Of their ten children those who weren't carried off by consumption in their early twenties were clearly bright but there was no free secondary schooling and they left school as soon as they could. They had learned poetry which my mother could still repeat to me and I in my turn learnt more in the infants and junior schools (five of them) which I attended. My mother herself periodically spent many months in various sanatoria with the family disease, propped up in bed in the healthy chill which was then the only treatment, reading, and writing to me. When we were reunited, either briefly on a visit or when she was let out to take up our life together for a few more years, it was books and reading that we shared, that and her passion that I should 'get on'.

My first efforts were recited to my cousin who hated poetry but indulged me. At twelve, now strongly under the influence of Keats and Milton and having passed the scholarship so that all the kingdoms of the world were in theory there before me, I decided to be a writer. Once again no one in our family had ever done such a thing and I realised I must keep it secret. Working class children, especially bastards, who were lucky enough to get to the grammar school were expected to go for security and respectability: to become teachers like my cousins. Artists, the arts and intellectuals were frowned on and dismissed with contempt as pretentious, inclined to baring their souls in public, 'bohemians'. Quite deliberately I played the game until my mother died two years later and I struck out against the fierce opposition of the rest of the family who were worried about my future if I went down this uncharted byway. Meanwhile I monopolised the school magazine with my efforts moving from rhymed to cadenced verse under the influence of T.S. Eliot and my mother's death.

I published my first work outside the school magazine when I was seventeen, in the review *Adam*. At the same time, looking for a larger form than the lyric I began on my first play, about Charlemagne, abandoned when I went to King's College, London. Until now fiction hadn't greatly interested me. I had resented the diet of set book novels by Austen, the Brontës and Mrs Gaskell we had been fed as likely to be of interest to, and suitable for, girls. I found the women's lives cramped, and the traditional expectations depicted in them, depressingly restrictive, especially the emphasis on marriage and children. I wanted to write and live and love. *Vissi d'arte, vissi d'amore* indeed. It was only at university where I encountered James Joyce, Virginia Woolf and, by myself, Joyce Cary that I began to take some interest in fiction and find modern fiction as exciting as poetry or plays. I published two short stories in the college magazine, *Lucifer*.

In my last year, when I ought to have been thinking only of finals, I wrote a dramatic version of *Piers Plowman* set in a mid-Fifties microchip factory during a lay-off. I submitted it to an *Observer* competition to find new playwrights, and, although it didn't win, it got me into the Royal Court Writers' Group under the auspices of George Devine and William Gaskill and in company with, among others, Edward Bond, Arnold Wesker, John Arden and Anne Jellicoe. Encouraged I took a teaching job to support myself and wrote another four plays. *Pearson* my first, re-titled *The Lay-off,* won the City of London playwright's award and was staged by the Guildhall School of Music and Drama to the consternation of some of the city fathers who claimed they could see similar stuff in their own factories if they wanted to. And there I stuck. There were no more productions and, in spite of having found myself an agent, who indeed got me my first commission from Granada to write a play for television, there was a growing pile of forlorn scripts.

In 1961 I met a young editor from Hutchinsons who was in

charge of a list called New Authors and he began to badger me
to write a novel for his list. I felt I was getting nowhere with the
theatre and was desperate for an audience. I had given up my
teaching job on the strength of the TV commission and was living
in a houseboat on the Thames for cheapness. Although neither of
us knew whether I could write a publishable novel, I decided to
follow his suggestion and set about writing my first full length
work of fiction, embedding in it the two short stories I had published in the college magazine, which I suddenly saw could be
part of a much longer autobiographical work, and calling it after
one of them: 'That's How it Was'. It was published in 1962 and
treated with the critical kindness often shown to first novels. In
style it owed a lot to my theatre writing: working class in setting,
using a great deal of concrete imagery and a lot of dialogue. I was
determined not to write what was then the fashionable Hampstead
novel, which indeed portrayed a world I knew nothing about.

My second novel, *The Single Eye*, was based on my post-
graduation experiences as a teacher of English in Naples. It was
heavily criticised for what was seen as its too vivid realism; 'scrap-
ing the bottom of the barrel' one reviewer called it. But I already
felt that (for me at that time at least) I had exhausted the immediate possibilities of the linear narrative. I wanted something both
linguistically and structurally more exciting, like the fiction of Jean
Genet who was also both novelist and dramatist. I looked abroad
for writers who were doing the kind of things that interested me,
rather than to middle England. I hadn't given up all hopes of the
theatre. I never have and indeed I managed to get another three
plays staged professionally, the most successful being *Rites* at the
National Theatre still in its Old Vic home, and most recently in
1995 *The Masque of Henry Purcell* at the Southwark Playhouse.

My third novel began as a non-fiction project in a series of tape
recorded interviews with homosexual women. I soon discovered
that, without a degree in sociology or a similar discipline, no one
would publish a book by me on such a contentious subject. It was
the editor-owner of a small, some thought sensationalist, publishing house, Anthony Blond, who suggested I should use the
material in a novel. He even offered to pay me £15 a week for as
long as it took to write. However when he began to suggest scenes
and characters that I should put in I declined, although I was desperate for money and taking every job, reviewing, reading for the
New Authors list and teaching evening classes, that I could get.

The origins of this novel gave me the chance I wanted to explore the use of different voices in fiction, with the result that when it was published in 1966 as *The Microcosm* it was described as 'wilfully experimental'.

Reader, I promise not to bore you with an account of every novel. (I have now published sixteen.) *The Microcosm*, because it was perceived as sensational, was my best seller. More importantly, having broken out of linear narrative, from then on I felt free to attempt something different with each new book and to follow a literary life of constant exploration of form, voices and genres.

When I first began to write fiction and was trying to live by my writing, apart from during my eighteen months on the houseboat, a First World War naval pinnace, I rented a series of unattractive flats and rooms that I felt disinclined to shut myself up in all day. I discovered that I could write anywhere, anywhere that is except at home or in a library, so I would take myself into central London from whichever dismal suburb I was then able to afford, and alternate between coffee bar and pub until I had done my day's stint which was as near a thousand words as I could make it before I ran out of juice.

To a large extent this early training has stayed with me. I still write as I did then on my knee in a notebook, not, unless I'm forced to, in my study, which is the place where I keep books, try to restrain papers from flooding into every other room, and do little bits of typing, but in an armchair or on a sofa in a light sitting room. Nowadays I do however need quiet without the distraction of conversation, actual or telephonic, radio or the jukebox I used to be able simply to shut out. I do find that ten minutes with a newspaper when I first sit down helps to concentrate my mind.

The notebook, in which indeed this is being written, is A4, wide spaced with margin and a side opening. The medium is ink from a cartridge pen. I write on the facing page only, keeping its left hand neighbour for insertions, second thoughts. Encircling fence lines like cartoon balloons, and arrows, show where these are to go into the main text. Each morning, as close to eight-thirty as I can make it, I read through and correct with Tippex what I have done the day before and write my insertions. Then I carry on until I can't do any more. I write bunched into a knot of concentration with a strong physical sensation of tense energy being expended until the last drop seems to be exhausted and I switch off. Whether there is any real physical expenditure, or whether the sensation is merely a psychological impression, hitching me up to a set of electrodes could prove, and even so that might inhibit the very reactions it was trying to measure.

Usually I run out of steam rather conveniently at lunchtime, leaving me the afternoon for libraries, research, committees, reading and commenting on the slurry of papers that pours off the fax machine or through the letterbox every day from my various interests. Once or twice a year there's a competition to be judged and often there are readings or lectures to be prepared and speeches to be wrought up. I can remember a time when no writer of fiction read work to the public. Only poets did that. But increasingly it's expected that the writer will give readings as part of the promotional programme and readers seem to enjoy being read to and being able to ask questions about the work itself and the writing life.

I see and hear what is taking place in the fiction as I write like a play or film running in my head. I begin at the beginning and work systematically through to the end, plotting scenes or thematic material in a series of notebooks as I go along. When I first started writing novels I plotted intensively, chapter by chapter, probably out of anxiety, but I find now that I can hold much more in my head and don't need to map out every section obsessively.

There's a period that antedates the putting down of the first sentence, a time of gestation from the very first glimmering of an idea, 'the hand-sized cloud', that may last a few months or over a year. I find the first idea comes quite suddenly out of nothing, a donné, from a chance remark, perhaps not even addressed to me, a newspaper or broadcast report, which begins to accrete like the piece of grit in the oyster or the sticky carapace of a caddis worm, organically, almost as if it's a natural unwilled process. It assumes a person, a character, a situation and a place. Perhaps I can make this clearer with an example. When *Illuminations* first came to me it was as an image of a woman, middle aged, alone in a cottage. The cottage was or had been mine but the woman was definitely not me. I began to wonder about her, to construct her life and character. At the same time it occurred to me that I wanted to write about the relationship of Britain to Europe, and I had an image of the Europa story as told by writers and painters, of the princess carried away by the bull. I thought the woman I could see alone in her cottage might go to Europe and fall in love. Her name I decided was Hetty.

During the gestation period, which is one of great excitement and pleasure, everything seems to feed into the book: daily news, personal events, exhibitions, music, the weather even. It's as if the mind has been flooded with a hyper-aesthesia inducing drug that gives the every-day a heightened resonance or as if a magnet were drawn across a field of coloured metal filings sucking them into a complex pattern. Suddenly, without warning, there arrived in the post a book called *Medieval Women Writers* sent by a friend in Cambridge who thought it would interest me. I had been looking-for another layer to my fictional sandwich. This chance happening gave me an historical story parallel to Hetty's, based on three letters in the book, translated from Latin, written home from Saxony by an eighth-century English nun who had gone there as a missionary with her mother. Now I had two distinct voices, periods and narratives which I could weave together to give the kind of density, richness and mutual illumination that sustains my pleasure in creation and keeps me writing on to the end.

The last week or so of gestation is spent obsessively trying the opening sentence over in my head to find the right tone, the right voice. Then one day I know I have it and that the next morning I must sit down and write it out. I believe with Dickens and Katherine Mansfield, to name only two, that the first sentence should seize the reader in some way with an *Ancient Mariner* grip. By the time I reach the point of actually beginning to write I will probably know the last sentence as well, the working title, the main characters, many scenes and set pieces, the themes and what I want to do with the language. All this will exist in note form in the books and be added to and re-read from time to time to remind myself of my original intention. I do leave myself considerable white space between the notes though, for invention and play or I should become bored and stale as the months pass, with something that was too programmatic.

While I'm working on a book I live parallel lives: in daily reality and in the virtual reality of the book, of the imagination, as if I'd put on those 3D goggles that we're told will give us the freedom to step out of our space and time into another dimension: the faery land of Tir na N'Og. So strong is the pull of this other world that when the book is finished and I take off the magic glasses that let you see with the mind's eye, I feel bereft. The last section of a novel is for me very intense and concentrated, a scherzo movement like, I imagine though I've never done it, slaloming downhill against the clock. At the end when that held tension slackens I feel not just bereft but always exhausted and often rather ill.

I do only one draft, correcting as I've said every morning and I often send off the book in chunks to my typist as I go along so that I have the continuing encouragement of a growing stack of neat pages, and with luck there will be only the last ten thousand words to be typed up at the end. It's important for me to have little devices like this, and keeping a word count, to combat the exhaustion and despair that set in from time to time as the months pass, to keep walking the tightrope to the very end. Every writer has some psychological support system and it's important to find what works for you. Self doubt is inevitable. Can I still do it? Who wants it anyway? My language is too dull, flashy, dry. Add your own debilitating adjectives to this list.

When the last pages come back I take a deep breath and sit down to read through the whole book and make further corrections. This is a process done on a kind of automatic pilot, of craftsmanship. By this stage there's nothing radical I can do to change my novel. It has acquired its own inevitability. It is; and like Pilate I've written what I have written. But this correcting of the whole typescript does give me the chance to pick any missed 'fleas out of the cat's fur' as Rosalind Belben has so cleverly and precisely described this process. This nit-picking is meant to remove previously unspotted repetitions, excessive adjectives and adverbs, words that chimingly rhyme, faulty cadences, monotonous rhythms, sentences that lose momentum and need breaking up, over writing, including for example the underlining comment to something already embodied in action or dialogue and therefore excess to requirements, redundant.

The next stage is to send copies to my agent with whom I've been for thirty-five-years and whose opinion is very important to me, and to the commissioning editor. Usually the editor, and there have been many over the years as they or I moved publishing house, comes back with comments and queries. Taking another deep breath I work carefully through these considering, accepting or rejecting. Then I return this, for me, final text which, these days, will next pass under the pedantic eye of a copy-editor, not at all the same function as the television editor of similar title, who will usefully check the spelling, query my punctuation and sometimes attempt to replace carefully cadenced and original phrasing with a near equivalent supposedly 'more accessible to the reader'.

Copy-editors often seem to be patronizing this putative reader. They profess to know what will be accessible to him, or more likely her, they assume in the case of a writer perceived in these days when everything must have a label or niche, as female, forgetting or perhaps never having heard Aphra Behn's claim for freedom for 'the masculine part the poet in me'. I have to say that I have no idea who my readers are, except that there were forty thousand of them last year through the public library system alone. Nor do I wish to know, although I'm very happy when they come up after a reading and tell me how much they've enjoyed my books over the years and ask me not to stop. I'm glad too that no one has yet done a statistical breakdown of them by age, sex and class as I suppose will be possible in the very near future.

Occasionally a reader will indicate a constituency I am said to represent, or sometimes the opposite. I remember once being attacked violently by a woman who said I had done 'nothing for women'. There's also the often encountered response when people outside the book world are told that you are a writer: 'I've never heard of you. Should I have read anything of yours? What do you write?' It's as though in some way this anonymity is the writer's fault, and also that we should apologize for doing what we do, as if it's a secret vice, a piece of self indulgence instead of an activity that sustains a multi-billion pound industry and thousands of jobs. This seems to me a very British attitude towards artists, intellectuals and culture in general.

I would like to think that if representation comes into it at all, and it certainly doesn't during the actual writing of a book, that I represent the widest constituency of all: humankind. Writing is for me a balancing act between the particular and the universal. The universal has to be clothed in the particular for it to become visible (airy nothings still need a local habitation), and yet without some universal armature the particular can be merely trivial and ephemeral. We have more in common as people than our social, cultural, geographical and general differences sometimes lead us to suppose. How else could we respond to any work by a 'foreign' author even in translation?

Particularly restricting is the term 'gay writer' which suggests only one theme and a potential audience of the same gender, half of a notional ten percent of the population. I don't believe British readers are so limited in their range of interest and sympathy that

they really wish us to write for and be read by a constituency
which is our own mirror image in age, sex, class, race and erotic
preference, for our own tribe within a tribe within a tribe until we
vanish like the mythical oozlum bird.

While writing fiction I read only non-fiction and that mostly
related in some way to my current book. A lot of research may
need to be done in the course of a book and, for example, locations, settings for scenes, visited or culled from guide books with
the help of maps. For my novel before last, *Occam's Razor*, I read
accounts of the Spanish Civil War, of the Second World War
British imprisonment of aliens, studied the video of a friend's
wedding, consulted Irish and Italian dictionaries, a chess manual,
and boned up on how to make electrical and explosive devices;
visited a cemetery, an encampment of the homeless, a soup
kitchen and a selection of charity shops as well as making the
almost routine, I find, study of maps. I always need to know
much more background than will appear in the final pages which
rest like an iceberg tip on a submerged two thirds of material that
supports the visible apex, the text.

For me it's important not only to get things right but to be able
to visualise actions in settings clearly myself in order to be able to
recreate them in as many dimensions as possible. In the case of a
novel called *I Want To Go To Moscow* I wanted an episode set in
an abattoir. Being a vegetarian I wasn't about to visit one even for
purposes of authenticity and connive at the deaths taking place
there. A manual designed for the butchery trade had to do in all
its hideous matter-of-factness. So intense is my absorption while
I'm writing that I felt quite ill describing the slaughterhouse in
detail as my protagonists went through it and only perked up
when the fictional flames began to consume it.

The following two pages show the manuscript original and the
final printed text of the opening of *Illuminations*. Because of the
gestation process I've described there are almost no changes to
this page as it was first put down: one word whited out, a few
insertions and two thirds down the page a word count just to reas-
sure me that I'm keeping to my usual number of words to a page.
Only eighty-nine thousand, nine hundred and sixty-five to go. Oh
yes, and there's the opening sentence deliberately inculcating a
feeling of mystery. 'The fox begins it.' Begins what? Which fox?
Why? And then at once Hetty's name, and she opens the back
door on the present tense and death.

the fox begins it. Hatty doesn't know this as she opens the back door on a little summer morning luminous as prelapsarian Eden where each leaf on the holly tree is a polished heliograph. Afterwards, looking back, she'll remember that this is the brushmark in the margin saying 'Start here', but now it's only a fox beached with its nose against the bootscraper grid as if it had run to her door to die, couldn't run any more because the nylon noose has cut deep into its throat, severed its neck. For a moment she's afraid as if it's a portent, the day overcast, & perhaps someone's left it there. Meaning what? And though she doesn't believe in them she thinks of witchcraft & the trappings of malice.

Then she sees that the rusty coat is sewn with seed pearls of dew & the smooth black lips, drawn back in a desperate snarl of terror & pain. If she had known could she have saved it? She bends down to look closer & sees that any intervention she might have made would have been too late. It's a young fox. She can't tell what sex and now she'll have to bury it before the sun brings out the flies. But not until she's given herself some breakfast strength while the problem adjusts itself in her mind to the practical where & how & whether she should remove the snare & the decomposition of that last into the daily murfie shrivelled by the sunlight.

She shuts the door on the morning & the heavy lump of death on her back doorstep & turns to put on the kettle & assemble cereal & milk & orange juice on the pine table where she can sit & munch, looking out at the front hedge of blackthorn where sparrows have begun the daily round of indignant chirp & flaunt. Predatory Reynard has got his come-uppance sneaking down to drowsing henfolk. The snare was meant for rabbit or

THE FOX begins it. Hetty doesn't know this as she opens the
back door on a late summer morning luminous as pre-lapsarian
Eden where each leaf on the holly tree is a polished heliograph.
Afterwards, looking back, she'll remember that this is the brush
mark in the margin saying, 'Start here', but now it's only a fox
beached with its nose against the bootscraper grid as if it had
run for dear life to her door to die, couldn't run away any more
because the nylon noose has cut deep into its throat and half
severed its neck. For a moment she's afraid as if it's a portent,
the day overcast, and perhaps someone's left it there. Meaning
what? And though she doesn't believe she thinks of witchcraft
and the trappings of malice.

Then she sees that the rusty coat is sewn with seed pearls of
dew and the smart black lips are drawn back in a desperate snarl
of horror and pain. If she had known could she have saved it?
She bends down to look closer and sees that any intervention
she might have made would have been too late. It's a young fox.
She can't tell what sex, and now she'll have to bury it before the
sun brings out the flies. But not until she's given herself some
breakfast strength while the problem adjusts in her mind to the
practical where and how and whether she should remove the
snare, and before the desperation of that last run into the dark
is shrivelled by the sunlight.

—1—

John Harvey

Easy Money? Writing for a Living

Immediately prior to writing this essay, I was working on the revisions to *Easy Meat,* the eighth in a projected sequence of ten Nottingham-based crime novels featuring Detective Inspector Charlie Resnick, and the ninety-fifth book I will have had published since 1975. Well, some of them were quite short and most of them were written very fast! Too fast. The most rudimentary spelling check aside (all those westerns in which I consistently misspelt *marshal* and *sheriff*) those early manuscripts would rarely have been dignified by anything as time-consuming and grand as serious revision. As Dashiell Hammett said about finishing a story, type 'THE END', stick it in an envelope and mail it out, forget about it till the cheque comes – and start the next.

I do intend to deal with how I began – how I progressed from the necessity of writing thirteen books a year to the ease and comfort of writing only one – but first I should like to go into some detail about the revisions I have just finished, the way I work now.

As I say, *Easy Meat* is part of a finite series: the first book, *Lonely Hearts* was published in 1989 by Viking, who also brought out the next four books – *Rough Treatment, Cutting Edge, Off Minor* and *Wasted Years* – at yearly intervals; in 1994 I moved to my current British publisher, Heinemann, who published *Cold Light* and then *Living Proof.* Each of these books has been published in the United States by Henry Holt, where my editor is Marian Wood, and this has led to a very interesting situation. For someone in my position – writing novels set and usually first published in this country – it is more usual, I think, for the English editor to have the major input into the books. Often, the US editor, buying American rights from the UK publisher or, as in this instance, through the agent direct, will do little more than baby-sit the volume through production. But the consistency of Holt's involvement, and their wholehearted support of the series, has meant that I have been able to make use of Marian Wood's considerable experience and understanding in the shaping of individual books and the sequence as a whole.

So, sitting down to commence work on my original draft of *Easy Meat*, I was armed with two versions of the manuscript: the one which Marian had read and annotated carefully, together with her two page letter discussing general points and a further nine pages of textual queries and suggestions; I also had another copy with copious notes from my editor at Heinemann, Louise Moore, along with a four page letter closely arguing specific improvements and changes. And I had a letter from my agent, Carole Blake, which included her comments and some detailed observations.

Now there is, of course, a potential problem here – all it would need is for one editor to be pulling one way, one in another, and my manuscript would be in danger of breaking apart under the strain. But the sequence and some of its characters are well-established, a basic style has been set and, anyway, I am in the hands of professionals prepared to find time to work on manuscripts at length. No longer the acknowledged norm!

In fact, what tends to happen is that where the notes on small points – removing a comma here, altering a word there – tend to be complementary and rarely overlap, those dealing with larger issues of plot, motivation and structure are more likely to point to the same areas of the text. So, in *Easy Meat*, both Louise and Marian agreed on the following: 1 – there was a slackness between chapters thirteen and twenty one which needed eliminating; 2 – the section of the plot to do with young people in care was lost from sight in the last quarter of the book, which made its reappearance at the end unsatisfactory; 3 – one of the emotional issues linking Resnick and a colleague was inadequately resolved; 4 – scenes showing one couple's relationship needed clarifying and sharpening; 5 – the recovery of one of the characters after a severe beating needed to be less miraculous, his re-introduction into the action more gradual; and 6 – too great a similarity in the names of some characters was confusing.

As it happened, all of these major points were ones I was happy to accept, that I had been half-aware of myself, and was prepared to find solutions to. Had this not been the case, I would most likely have gone through my normal process of flying off the handle and over-reacting, making it startlingly clear that there was absolutely no way in which I was going to agree to so-and-so or this-and-that, and then, having calmed down, seen there were grounds for compromise and discussion.

So slowly I set to work. And it was slow, or seemed slow to me, rewriting always does; and yes, there were times when I felt like dumping the whole mess out of the window and would go stomping out of the flat and off across Hampstead Heath, apple in hand and someone like Pulp pumping through the headphones of my Walkman. But then I would get back and make another cup of good coffee and spread the papers out before me. I wanted it to be right, as right as I could get it. You always do, and of course you always think it *is* and it comes as a shock – to me anyway – to realise the extent to which something which you thought was far and away the best thing you'd ever written, is so lax and sloppy and – Oh, God! – so wretchedly self-indulgent.

I cut. I think I'm good at cutting. I enjoy it. One of the things I was best at when I was at school (and I bet they don't teach it any more) was précis: for a writer it's a wonderful skill; for a teacher, also. It enabled me to guide students towards the heart of school and – briefly – university texts, and it's helped me to adapt the work of other writers as varied as A.S. Byatt and Arnold Bennett for radio and television. On a good day, when I'm con-centrating, it helps me to clear the clutter from my own work. So tightening that section between chapters thirteen and twenty one wasn't as difficult as it might sound; there were whole pages waiting to have my red pencil slashed through them.

To give some indication of what I'm talking about, here are two versions of a section from chapter thirteen. It's a fairly self-contained passage – Norma is treating herself to a lie-in on a Sunday morning, her thoughts shifting between past pleasures with the two significant men in her life, and present troubles, the worst of which is that her son, Nicky, has been arrested and is being held in secure accommodation.

EASY MEAT Chapter Thirteen

For Norma Snape, Sunday was the memory of waking late in that bed in Huddersfield, not a bed really, a mattress on the floor. Waking with a sore head and the sunlight patching across room, Patrick sitting propped on pillows beside her, building his first joint of the day. "Listen," Patrick would say. "Listen." Church bells tumbling heavy-footed around the rooftops; the set of chimes he had hung down by the window stirring in the breeze. "Here, take it." Lying there, getting more and more stoned until finally the munchies overcame them and one or other of them raided the refrigerator left-over pizza and chocolate chip ice cream. Once Patrick had run to the corner shop wearing swimming trunks, Jesus sandals and one of her blouses, to fetch half a dozen jumbo Mars Bars, a Mr Kipling treacle tart and three cans of Ambrosia Devon Custard. Al Green on the record player all the while: Let's Stay Together, Here I Am (Come and Take Me), Call Me (Come Back Home).

Or Sunday was being with Peter, curved on her belly, legs slightly parted, Peter's hands at her back like wings, barely touching, never still. Sheena, nine months old, fast asleep close alongside her, thumb in her mouth, hair, fair across her eyes. The rise and fall of the child's tiny chest no more than the delicate pressure of Peter's fingers at the base of her spine. The tension within her as she bit into the soft underside of her lip, waiting for his hands to move lower.

Sunday was here now, spinning dreams, the mug of tea she had fetched herself long since grown cold. The radio tuned to

EASY MEAT   *she thought she could*   Chapter Thirteen
                                    and nothing thouse   *how she would faint,*
                                                                                    from this
                                                                                        now

~~GEM AM and turned low. Sheena running herself a bath.~~ The sound of
the television faint from downstairs, though she'd swear that
~~She'd~~ heard Shane go out *either* off to spend the day with his mates from
Ilkeston like as not, A tight-mouthed lot, ~~never~~ a word between
~~them, civil~~ or the other kind, ~~hair~~ cropped short till it was
little more than stubble, eyes that looked through you as if you
weren't a ~~person,~~ weren't there.

        ~~Norma~~ *He* ~~fidgetted the sheet around her, reached for a~~
~~magasine.~~ *like* Nicky, he wasn't there, for certain. Shut up in that
place, poor bastard, that bastard home. This afternoon, she'd get
herself up nice, go out and see him, take him some chocolate,
cigarettes, something special, something for a treat. No matter
what he'd done, when it came down to it, he was her son; *there was* / no
getting away from that, no getting away from it at all. She'd just
stay there ten minutes longer, get up for good then, mash some
fresh tea. Norma reached out for and lit a cigarette, flicked
towards the problem page of ~~the~~ *her* magazine; anyone else's but her
own, they were a cinch.

        She was still lying there, half an hour later, when the
doorbell rang.

When it became clear that, whoever it was, they weren't going to
go away, Norma pulled on her dressing gown and shuffled to the
upstairs window, overlooking the street.

        "What the hell ... ?"

        She saw Resnick looking up at her and what she saw in his

growing inside him.

    "Lynnie, your dad's fine. Honest."

Her mother who believed in dreams.

For Norma Snape the best Sundays were not present but past. She
could remember when she was still with Patrick, waking late in
that bed in Huddersfield, sunlight patching across room and
Patrick sitting propped on pillows beside her, building his first
joint of the day. Then lying there, getting more and more stoned
until finally the munchies overcame them and ~~one or other of them~~ they
raided the refrigerator/ for left-over pizza and chocolate chip ice
cream. Al Green on the record player all the while: <u>Let's Stay
Together</u>, <u>Here I Am (Come and Take Me)</u>, <u>Call Me (Come Back Home)</u>.

    Or later, Sundays with Peter, his hands fluttering at her
back like wings, barely touching, never still. Sheena, nine months
old, fast asleep close alongside her, thumb in her mouth, hair
fair across her eyes. The rise and fall of the child's tiny chest
no more than the delicate pressure of Peter's fingers at the base
of her spine. The tension within her as she bit into the soft
underside of her lip, waiting for his hands to move lower.

    Norma stirred and reached for the mug of tea she had
fetched ~~herself~~ earlier and which had long since grown cold. Faint
from downstairs she could hear the sound of the television, though
she'd swear that she'd heard Shane go out, the best part of an hour ago
~~off to spend the day~~
~~with his mates from Ilkeston like as not.~~
    ~~Norma~~ She fidgetted the sheet around her and reached for a

108

magazine. She could hear Sheena now, running herself a bath. But
not her Nicky, he wasn't there, for certain. Shut up in that
place, poor little bastard, shut up in that bastard home. This
afternoon, she'd get herself up nice, go out and see him, take him
some chocolate, cigarettes, something special, something for a
treat. No matter what he'd done, when it came down to it, he was
her son; there was no getting away from that, no getting away from
it at all. She'd just stay there ten minutes longer, get up for
good then, mash some fresh tea. Norma ~~reached out for and~~ lit a
cigarette, flicked towards the problem page ~~of the magazine~~ —
anyone else's but her own, they were a cinch.

She was still lying there, half an hour later, when the
doorbell rang.

When it became clear that, whoever it was, they weren't going to
go away, Norma pulled on her dressing gown and shuffled to the
upstairs window, overlooking the street.

"What the hell ... ?"

She saw Resnick looking up at her and what she saw in his
eyes drove into her stomach like a fist.

Downstairs, she could see him silhouetted through the
mottled glass panels at the top of the door. Impatient with the
bolts, her fingers finally fumbled back the door.

"Norma ... "

It was till there in his eyes and in the way he stood.

"It's Nicky, isn't it?"

The first version is my original draft with Louise Moore's editorial comments – four small textual points and a broader suggestion; the crossings-out and additions are mine. What I'm aiming for is a cleaner line, something that is atmospheric but uncluttered. So that long list of foods has got to go – you see what I mean about self-indulgent and so have those church bells tumbling heavy-footed around the rooftops. Far too literary and self-conscious – it sounds as though I'd been listening to *Under Milk Wood* – and quite wrong for a section revolving around Norma's consciousness. I'll allow myself to keep the Al Green reference, though; it's already established that music was important to Norma's relationship with Patrick and, besides, music is very much a part of the texture of these books. I came close to throwing out the sentence about wings at the start of the second paragraph, for reasons similar to those which eliminated the tumbling bells, but in the end I decided it helped to show Peter's more ethereal, less corporeal nature – and, after all, it *is* Sunday. The tone in the final paragraph shifts closer into Norma's thought and speech patterns – it's internal mono-logue – and then pulls back again with the final sentence, which is where the outside – and bad news – intrude on her reverie. The effect, I hope, is one of closing in and then pulling away, and that kind of movement of tone is very much a part of the way I write.

Happy with my biroed changes, I made the alterations on the word processor and then printed them out; when the entire manuscript had been reworked, I read it through again and at that stage made the few additional changes shown in the second version, just cleaning up the text a little, honing it down.

My original draft of the novel was 480 double-spaced sheets of A4, fifty chapters in all; the revised draft was 464 pages and forty seven chapters. By my estimate, I cut between thirty-five and forty pages in order to tighten the manuscript, but then added twenty to twenty-five more in order to clarify plot and character-ization. The first draft took me some four months to write: that's working for between four and five hours for five or six mornings a week, without a significant break. The rewrites took between four to six weeks, but with a few days out here and there. Oh, and there is still the copy editing stage to come, to say nothing of the final proofs....

Writing is my job, my work; it's how I pay my bills. It's also what I do that keeps me sane and permits the rest of my life. There's a quotation from André Debus' story, 'Finding a Girl in

America', which is written out on a card near my desk, which ends, '...after a morning at the desk, he has earned his day on earth. When he did not work, except by choice, he disliked himself.' There's another quotation, from John Irving's *The World According to Garp* attached to the refrigerator – '"If you are careful," Garp wrote, "if you use good ingredients, and you don't take any shortcuts, then you can usually cook something very good. Sometimes it is the only worthwhile product you can salvage from a day: what you make to eat. With writing, I find, you can have all the right ingredients, give plenty of time and care, and still get nothing. Also true of love. Cooking, therefore, can keep a person who tries hard sane."'

Well, yes. Cooking, the light, listening to music, walking, really striding out, settling into the front row of the movies in the afternoon, reading other writers' work – all of those contribute towards keeping me sane. Contribute towards making it possible for me to write. Earn my living. Do my job.

I had been teaching English and Drama in Stevenage, something I'd been doing – and largely enjoying – there and in other schools for twelve years. Either I was going to start seriously applying for deputy headships and take on board that that was going to be the rest of my working life, or I was going to do something else.

I had no idea what. But my friend Laurence James lived near me and after a spell in publishing, Laurence was now a full-time freelance writer and whenever I went over to visit him I thought, wow, this looks like a pretty good life to me! He would get up in the morning and drink his coffee, glance at the papers, wander into his study and wind a fresh sheet of paper into the typewriter, sit there happily working, get up and fetch more coffee when he felt like it, pause to wander round the garden, chat on the phone, whatever. At the end of the day, Laurence's eight or ten pages were written and the following day he would get up and do the same. Laurence, I couldn't help noticing, seemed happy about all of this *and* he got paid. And paid pretty well. He liked the life so much that like most converts he was keen to proselytize. Try it, he said, what have you go to lose? Me, who had edited school and college newspapers and magazines, who had compiled and produced school plays based on improvisation, who had written articles about English teaching and too many bad poems; whose fear of writing fiction was that I would run out of ideas at page

twenty-seven. Thank the Lord for genre fiction! As far as the
beginning writer is concerned, the more firmly ensconced in the
genre the better. Idealess at page twenty-seven? Remember
Raymond Chandler's advice: when in doubt, have a man come
through the door with a gun in his hand. And so for four or five
genre-filled years I had men – and women – come through the
door astride chopped-down Harley Davidsons, brandishing toma-
hawks and AK47s, wearing twin pearl-handled Colt 45s holstered
low at the hip and wearing very little at all.

Thank the Lord for the boom in British paperback publishing
in the mid-seventies. Within my first year as a freelance writer, a
senior editor actually rang me at home one evening and asked if
I would be interested in writing a series of westerns for them. I
was, and it was called *Herne the Hunter*; in the event I co-wrote it
with Laurence James and it ran to number twenty-four and was
published in America, Germany and Greece as well as in Britain.
Together with Laurence and another editor-turned-writer, Angus
Wells, I did a lot of co-writing on western series. We would construct the main character and situation together, talk through
story lines and then retreat to write alternate books on our own.
To this day I can only tell which of William S. Brady's 'Hawks'
and 'Peacemakers' are mine by turning to the final paragraph; if
our hero wins out in an orgy of bloody gunplay, it's one of
Angus'; if it's downbeat and raining, it's probably mine.

Westerns, war books, teen romances – 50,000 words each and
a book every four weeks, sometimes less. It was great! I was being
paid to practice. Of course, when I look at most of these books
now I'm hard-pushed to find a sentence or two that I feel proud
of, though at the time I thought they were wonderful. They were
certainly the best I could do. You don't get – and this is a lesson
so many would-be writers who try to 'down-market' themselves
in search of cheques and letters of acceptance have to learn –
published by writing badly on purpose. It may be a kind of trash
but it has to be good trash. You have to like it.

Specifically, what did I learn?

Four things.

One: how to pace a narrative so that the reader wants to turn
the page. I can't explain this clearly. But it's to do with fulfiling
the generic expectations for incident and surprise; it's to do with
making motivation and character clear enough to understand; it's
to do with satisfying one part of the reader's curiosity about what

is going to happen to one or other of the main protagonists, while setting in motion another set of doubts or directions.

Two: how to let a story evolve organically, to allow it room to breathe. I have almost never worked from a tight and pre-determined plan. I don't outline in detail, especially now. What I do begin with is a central idea, which is often a combination of story and theme. (For instance, the suicide of a young person whilst in care triggers off both, *is* the root of both.) Sue Grafton has a wonderful metaphor for writing, which is that it is like driving in fog. Some days you can see fifty yards, some five; but you carry on driving and trust that as you advance the road will clear before you. I think it's true. When it's going well the straight ride is exhilarating; sometimes there are crossroads and byways to explore, and occasionally one of these is a dead end and you will have to backtrack, but the excitement for a writer – as for the reader – is in the journey. If the route is too familiar, the scenery is the same as has been described before, there is no freshness, no surprise. Jazz, someone said, is the sound of surprise. Good writing, likewise.

Three: how to write dialogue and how to let it do the work, carry the story. Dialogue used to be the worst thing I did. I couldn't have a character say something as simple as, "Yes," or"Maybe," without it sounding wooden and false. I would try to avoid using dialogue at all and editors would send manuscripts back instructing me to get some more white onto the page – all of that dense, unbroken black was off-putting to my potential readers. I learned by going to the movies, closing my eyes and listening; reading writers whose dialogue sang and listening. Ross Thomas. Elmore Leonard. George V. Higgins. Let the characters reveal themselves through what they say; let the story unfold through what people say. First you listen and then you write it down: if your characters aren't talking then most likely they haven't come to life yet. And until they talk they never will.

Four: not to wait for inspiration. It *is* a job. I like to do it almost every day. There's a rhythm you settle into, a rhythm for each book, and if you ignore it for too long you lose it. Don't make excuses, make time; sit down in whatever space you use, behind whatever machine. Maybe you didn't quite finish this chapter or section yesterday, so you already know what you need to do today; if you did come to the end of that chapter and you're not quite sure where to continue, don't sit there and fiddle, re-type the last couple of pages of the previous day's work, get back into the rhythm, the feel, relax into the flow. It'll come, it'll come, trust it. On those rare occasions that it doesn't, don't beat yourself up: go for a walk, go off to a movie, pull down that recipe for baked cod *en cassoulet* you've been meaning to try, or the salad with anchovies and chick peas; go on, what are you waiting for?

Notes on Contributors

Adam Thorpe was born in Paris in 1956 and brought up in India, Cameroon and England. He has published three volumes of poetry, the most recent being *From the Neanderthal* (Cape, 1999) and three novels – *Ulverton* (Secker, 1992), *Still* (Secker, 1995) and *Pieces of Light* (Cape, 1998). His first collection of short stories, *Shifts*, was published by Cape in January 2000. He is the author of several plays for BBC Radio and a stage play. He lives in France with his wife and three children.

Catherine Fisher's first novel, *The Conjuror's Game* was short-listed for the Smarties Prize. She is also the author of the acclaimed *Snow-Walker* trilogy and *The Candleman*, which won the Tir na nOg Prize in 1995. *The Lammas Field* (Hodder) and a third collection of poems, *Altered States* (Seren) appeared in 1999. The third volume in an ongoing fantasy series, *The Book of the Crow – Flain's Coronet –* is due from the Bodley Head in 2000.

Mark Illis has written three novels, *A Chinese Summer*, *The Alchemist* and *The Feather Report*, all published by Bloomsbury. His short stories have appeared in many magazines and anthologies. He is currently writing for television and working on a new novel.

Penelope Fitzgerald's *Gate of Angels* was published in 1990 by HarperCollins. Published by the same company in 1995, *The Blue Flower* won the Heywood Hill Award in 1996 and the United States Critics Circle Award in 1998. In 1999 Ms Fitzgerald was awarded the Golden Pen by the London branch of International PEN, for 'distinguished services to literature'. Sadly, she died in April just as this book went to press.

Wilson Harris was born in Guyana. His work includes *The Guyana Quartet* (160-63), *Tumatumari* (1968), *The Sleepers of Roraima* (1970), *Black Marsden* (1972), *Companions of the Day* *and Night* (1975), *The Carnival Trilogy* (1985-90), *Resurrection at Sparrow Hill* (1993) and *Jonestown* (1996). His criticism includes *The Radical Imagination* (1992) and *Selected Essays* (1999). He was awarded the Premio Mondello dei Cinque Continenti in 1992.

Christopher Meredith is a prize-winning poet and novelist. His three novels are *Shifts* (1988), *Griffri* (1991) and *Sidereal Time* (1998, all Seren). He lives in Brecon and lectures at the University of Glamorgan.

Jennifer Johnston is the author of ten novels, most recently *The Illusionist* (1995). Her books have won several prizes and have been shortlisted for several more, including the Booker Prize, and five – *How Many Miles to Babylon?, Shadows on Our Skin, The Old Jest, The Railway Stationman* and *The Christmas Tree* – have been adapted for television. All her novels have been translated into several European languages.

Caryl Phillips's most recent book is *The Atlantic Sound,* an exploration of the slave trade in England, Ghana and America. His work has been televised, and *Crossing the River* was shortlisted for the 1993 Booker Prize and won the James Tait Black Memorial Prize.

Maureen Duffy's huge bibliography includes novels, plays, volumes of poetry, biographies and social history. She has been President of the Writers' Guild of Great Britain, Chairman of the Authors' Lending and Copyright Society and is Vice President of the European Writers' Congress and of the British Copyright Council.

John Harvey's sequence of ten Resnick novels finished with *Last Rites* (1998). *Now's the Time,* the collected Resnick stories, was published in 1999.

Maura Dooley is a poet and freelance arts worker. Her collections include *Explaining Magnetism* and *Kissing a Bone* and her anthology *Making for Planet Alice* (all Bloodaxe Books) were Poetry Book Society Recommendations. *Kissing a Bone* was shortlisted for the T.S. Eliot Prize. Currently she is editing *The Honey Gatherers: love poetry* (for Bloodaxe) due in 2000.